Tex Smith's Hot Rod History

BOOK ONE: THE BEGINNINGS

by Tom Medley

TRACING AMERICA'S MOST POPULAR
AUTOMOTIVE HOBBY

Printed and bound in the United States of America

First published in 1990 by Motorbooks International Publishers & Wholesalers, PO
Box 2, 729 Prospect Avenue, Osceola, WI 54020 USA

Created by Tex Smith Publishing Co. PO Box 726, 29 East Wallace, Driggs, ID 83422
PHONE (208) 354-8133   FAX (208) 354-8137

Library of Congress Cataloging-in-Publication Data

Medley, Tom
    Hot rod history/ from the editors of Hot rod mechanix.
        p.   cm.
    ISBN 0-87938-477-8 : $17.95
    1. Hot rods—History I. Hot rod mechanix
TL236.3.H68 1990
629.228—dc20   90-37743
                                                   CIP

Printed and bound in the United States of America

Contents

TEX SMITH PUBLISHING
29 East Wallace, PO Box 726, Driggs, Idaho 83422

Publisher	LEROI TEX SMITH
Author	TOM MEDLEY
Editor	RICHARD JOHNSON
Art Director	BOB REECE
Art Assitant	VICKY DAVIDSON
Copy Editor	BECKY JAYE
Office Manager	JANET SMITH

Printed And Bound In the United States

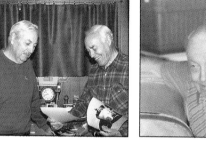

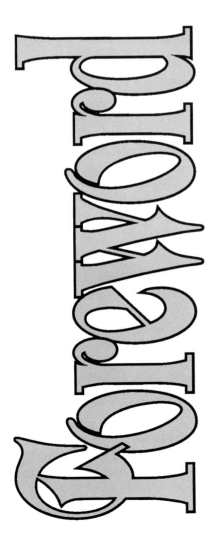

Wow! Time (and A-V8s) does fly. It seems only yesterday that I was loading the trunk of a roadster with sleeping bag, an old insulated Coke picnic box loaded with bologna sandwiches and Grapette, and a box of assorted hand-me-down tools, the intention being a day at the dry lakes. And here we are, doing a book on hot rod history.

But not just any history. A genuine, eye-witness history, through the eyes of those people who lived it. Geeesh, are we getting old, or something?

A few short years ago, I was helping chart the course of an antique automobile magazine/newspaper, and in general being immersed in restored cars. I was, from every vantage point, involved with automotive history. I didn't realize then that hot rodding was beginning to get a grey beard, that it was getting on in years, that before long we would be looking back (as a collective group of enthusiasts) and saying "remember when?"

So, here we are, in the 1990s, thinking back over 7 decades of hot rodding. To times before some of us were born, to times that some of us consider the "Golden Age" of hot rodding, to times that seem only yesterday to us ... and ancient history to others.

Yes, by all accounts, hot rodding has reached an age of remembrance. Not of bench racing, but of trying to establish a record, a correct record. A history.

In recent years, I have talked with many rodders of advancing age who bemoan the fact that we have let some of our pioneers slip into this history without getting their stories. The Winfields, and the Edelbrocks, and the Schieffers, and the Weiands, and hundreds more. People who did things and made decisions that may be with the hobby/sport for as long as such a hobby/sport exists. Truthfully, the fault is ours, all of us who participate in hot rodding. We should all be keeping journals and taking our share of snapshots, and recording our share of the tales from others. Of course, we don't, and we probably won't in the future. Which is why this book is before you.

About 15 years ago, I began the tedious project of gathering Information and photos about hot rodding. The longer and deeper I became involved in the search, the farther back in time went the so-called "beginning of hot rodding." Finally, I became convinced that the very first self-propelled vehicle (automobile) must surely have been a hot rod. If we consider the definition of a hot rod as a personalized, improved performance vehicle. To be sure, almost as soon as the first production car hit the road, someone started stripping it down for greater speed.

But, if we are to place a convenient Beginning on the sport, we would probably agree that all this started sometime in the early 1920s. When track racing became popular all across America, when any person could modify a Model T or Chevy 4 engine, when racing and hot rodding were inseparable.

With this in mind, we went hunting information. But we chose wisely in sending forth our chief scout. We asked Tom Medley to create our very first Hot Rod History, and we call it Book One. Because Tom Medley was heavy into hot rodding in the 1930s. Because he became an ace photographer for Hot Rod Magazine in the late '40s, and because he knows first-hand most of the legends in the sport.

But doing a history is a mind-boggling task. A number of years ago, one of the historians of hot rodding embarked on writing a hot rod history. It took only a few short weeks to convince him that such a duty was akin to writing a history of the world. Too much to record in too few pages. A couple of years ago, Don Montgomery published the first of two books on history, outstanding hardcover volumes that we heartily recommend (Motorbooks has them available) as a part of your ongoing collection.

Through all of this, however, we stuck to our guns on the kind of history we wanted to do. We wanted a history that was a photographic compilation of events. Lots of pictures, just enough words. Something endlessly fun to browse, yet something full of information. For now, and for those yet to come. But we wanted this to be from a personal standpoint. We wanted those who lived it to tell and show about it.

To this end, Tom Medley called on his legion of friends. Could he go visit and look through the photo album? And could he take photos of those old photos? Finally, could he do some short interviews?

In every case, the answer was a resounding "Absolutely!" In fact, as word of Tom's hunt began to spread around west coast hot rodding circles, long-ago acquaintances began to call and offer assistance. Before long, it became evident that one book simply would not do the job. Nor will two, or three. Therefore, there is no planned end to the Tex Smith HOT ROD HISTORY series. We'll do them until history runs out.

This history series won't be exactly the same with each book, but our aim consistently will be to give to the hobby what it deserves ... an honest review. History is always colored by the experiences of the historian, but in our case, we want the historian to be the person who was involved. We want to get away from the middleman if we can, and I think you'll agree that we have succeeded admirably with this first edition of HOT ROD HISTORY.

Oh, there are bound to be discrepancies. Dates, places, names ... all of these fade with time. But hopefully, what we will do is jog the memories of other participants to an event. Eventually, this collective memory should serve to get the record(s) as straight as possible.

Most of all, we want to help generate an interest in the history of America's innovative, dynamic, imaginative automotive past. Not the past of the automakers, but the past of the auto-users, those people who have helped to catapult the American car to such a pinnacle of utility that no future history of civilization will be able to ignore the part played by the automobile in mankind's march to destiny.

And, through it all, we want this to be a history that is fun. Fun for you, and fun for those people who are remembering and sharing.

An Historic photo of Tex Smith (the tall one is him).

LeRoi Tex Smith
Publisher

PS: Are we interested in history from your point of view? You bet! If you have been involved in the hobby/sport for a number of years, and you feel you can share in making a more complete record, send us your story. Include photographs with captions, but please, don't send us photos that are irreplaceable. We don't want to chance losing valuable documents. Instead, have copies of valued photos made and send the copies. Dates, names, places: These need to be included when known. Thanx a bunch.

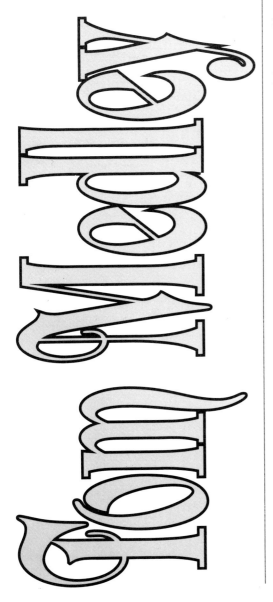

(PUBLISHER'S NOTE: When we were surveying the crowd for our history book author, one name kept blaring in headline type. Tom Medley. An accomplished writer, editor, photographer, and artist, Tom was/is the perfect man for the job. Born in Oregon in 1920, Medley has been astride the hot rod sport all his life, so without further ado ....)

TEX: When did you get really involved in rodding?

TOM: Back in the Thirties, up where I lived near Salem, Oregon. There was a lot of activity up there then, which seems peculiar to anyone away from the west coast. But in those days, guys were always coming and going, from Seattle to Los Angeles, so ideas about cars moved freely. We had a lot of people building circle track cars, some of them really super full-blown racers, but most of them modified stockers. Almost everything was an open-top car, T's and A's and the like. Of course, after the war (World War II), the midgets really came on big for a while.

Anyway, I started seeing fixed up Fords and Chevys. There wasn't a huge difference in our minds between a custom and a rod, since we were working on mostly the same stuff. A custom might be a 1936 Ford with fender skirts, but the same car would be a rod. It wasn't until many years later that we started separating the two building ideas.

TEX: As I recall, in those earlier days, you spent some time working in an upholstery shop.

TOM: That's where I learned to do trim work and why I still have a sewing machine out in the garage. Once you learn something like upholstery, you don't forget it easily. Anyway, at that shop I saw a lot of the special cars built in the northwest. I guess it was just a natural interest in cars. I know that many rodders worked as mechanics and bodymen or painters, so this interest in cars just seems to gravitate a person toward hot rodding and racing.

TEX: But you didn't have a car when you first came to California?

TOM: No, not when I came down to Fullerton Junior College before the war. I got a scholarship to the college to play basketball, and I would hitch hike down and back. It was a long way, going by thumb, but it's still a long way by modern car. Of course, I passed through all the neat steelhead fishing country where you and I like to spend time, so it wasn't so bad.

TEX: Like most everyone, you got caught up in the war.

TOM: In the army, and ended up in Europe. But not in the motorpool, like Wally Parks. You hear about Parks hopping up Jeeps just so they could climb the big mountains in the Philippines? I was always interested in music, and somehow I ended up working with the entertainment groups that came over. Like all the other GIs, I was always showing off pictures of my hot rod back home.

TEX: And after?

TOM: I went back to Oregon and to doing upholstery. In there somewhere, I got interested in photography, so when Bob Petersen introduced Hot Rod Magazine in 1948, I was ready to send in photos and artwork. After a few issues of HRM, I was offered a job on the staff. It wasn't much of a staff, and Eric Rickman and I used to carry issues of Hot Rod down to Ascot Stadium to sell them in the stands.

TEX: So when did Stroker show up?

TOM: Along about the first year, but if you go back and look at Stroker McGurk, you see the cartoon character evolve. You remember that I also did a cartoon for Cycle Magazine about that time, called Flat-Out Snodgrass.

Check the normal-height '32 roadster in the background and then scope the channeled "C" class '32. Quite a difference in frontal area. El Mirage just after WWII. Owned by Jerry Stroner.

TEX: Yeah. I've got some of those old originals on the wall, along with some Stroker originals. I rescued them from the PPC trash can years ago. I wish I had kept all those doodles of Stroker you've papered cafes across the west coast with.

TOM: Well, Stroker kind of served as the alter-ego for hot rodders everywhere. And it was probably just coincidence that a lot of things Stroker did in the cartoon eventually appeared in real life hot rodding. Like the drag chute. Usually, ideas for the cartoon would come from a bull-session with other guys, but they wouldn't know they were giving me ideas.

TEX: Some of those sessions we had at HRM in the Fifties and Sixties sure led to strange results, but they also helped make the magazine the leader. You got into the advertising department along in there, as I remember.

TOM: Uh-huh, and eventually I moved over to become editor of Rod & Custom. Spence Murray and Lyn Wineland had been there, and I took over in the mid-Sixties. That's when we started to see a new look emerging in the hobby. Parks had left HRM to direct NHRA full time, and we could see drag racing becoming more and more a professional sport. But street rodding, or traditional hot rodding as you always called it, was beginning to spread. So, we started to kind of make the sport a lot more visible in R&C.

TEX: Well, Rod & Custom had always been a kind of kid's magazine, especially with the small format, and it really didn't have a definitive image.

TOM: No, so we started doing a lot of street rod coverage. We did those vintage tin articles from you, and it all just seemed to come together.

TEX: Didn't R&C get up to about 130,000 circulation monthly in the late Sixties?

TOM: I think so. We had Bud Bryan on staff, and artists, the whole thing. Not like the one-man show that Pat Ganahl has to put up with now.

TEX: But this is a history about the earlier days. You did a lot of the early photography at HRM.

TOM: And we did some early movies, like up at Bonneville. We even did some hot rod records with Scatman Caruthers, which is a sidenote that I'll bet

very few people remember. We did car stuff a lot of years before the Beach Boys.

TEX: It was a bunch different from today.

TOM: I'll say. We were doing the magazine with the old hot lead type. We were using those old heavy cameras. A lot different. I like today much better.

TEX: So, early on, you had to visit with all of the builders and shops that have become legends?

TOM: That was the only way we could get information. And most of the shops were little hole-in-the-wall places, or the guy's backyard garage. It was the same everywhere, in southern California as well as Indy. In fact, we were involved with a lot of people who later became famous at Indy or on international race tracks. They all seemed to start the same way. Maybe it was a good learning experience, but since we didn't know any other way, it was the only way. I'll tell you one thing, some of those guys were real craftsmen. And they did it without all the fancy stuff the guys today have.

TEX: I know. I really get tired hearing people say that the rods and race cars we built back then were bad.

TOM: There were some really outstanding cars built. Not a lot of them have survived, though.

TEX: Ok, I'll let you go. I gotta get to a trout lake, and I know you are planning another Alaska foray. But, finish this book first!

The old master, Karl Orr, changes manifolds on this Karl and Veda roadster during a pre-war lakes meet. Veda Orr was the only gal running the lakes at that time.

Ed "Axle" Stewart and Nellie Taylor in Ed's '32. Ed was the father of the "Dropped Dago" axle.

Karl Orr in his Cragar-powered modified car turned a strong 126.65 mph before WWII.

Bruce Blair's (Don's brother) '23 "T" V8 roadster, complete with "huffer". Note juice brakes all around.

Tom Medley in a time warp, atop the fender of his "custom" 1936 Ford roadster, with skirts and Oregon plates. Scene was day lakes meet in southern California at a time when tom was breaking in to Hot Rod Magazine as photographer. Those who know Tom well claim little has changed through the years, except that now he has a wild 1940 Ford coupe hot rod.

Arnold Birner in his 4-port Riley-powered '29 roadster. This car never clocked, but the engine ran 125.06 mph in a modified.

How about this trick rear-engined '29 roadster. It created quite a stir in its first outing at the lakes before the war.

Full-fendered "T" V8 5-window coupe at the Russetta meet, El Mirage, California in 1949.

Below-Glendale Coupe and Roadster Club chopped and channeled "B" class sedan. Turned 112.21 mph at the Russetta meet in 1949.

Left-George Spear's '32 chopped 3-window. A typical post-war lakes coupe.

James Bowers' channeled "C" class '34 Ford coupe at the 1949 Russetta meet at El Mirage Dry Lake.

This super nice '32 Roadster drove all the way to the '53 Bonneville meet from Ashtabula, Ohio. Note the quick-change rear end.

A typical '32 full-fendered coupe seen on the streets of southern California in 1954. Check those monster whitewalls and "snap-on" wires, right on for the time.

A super clean street/drag strip roadster owned by Al Knoll of Bell, California. The '29 Ford body is mounted on '32 rails. Fenders are '32 Ford.

Beautiful Bonneville Mabee "Street Liner" ready for a quick pass down the long black line. How about those Mercedes batwing doors? The car was built by Denny Larson.

This tail job didn't have far to come to go racing as he's from Salt Lake City, just an hour or so down the road. Starter Higbee gives the driver instructions. Dean Moon is with the camera.

Below-Tom's GMC engine runs Howard's cam, rocker arms and injectors. Tom was a GCRC Club member and brick layer by trade.

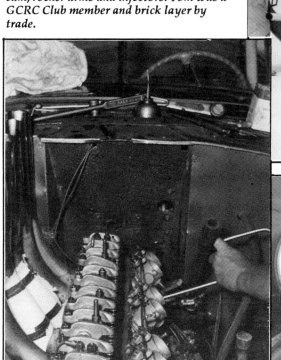

Howard Johansen (Howard's Cams) running an early OHV engine on his dyno. Howard could make any engine put out that extra horsepower. One of the sport's top competitors.

The noisiest car of the Russetta meet in June 1951 was Tom "Akmo" McLaughlin's GMC-powered Cord sedan. Speed was 124.13 mph.

Tom "Akmo" McLaughlin's 1941 Ford tudor set a new Russetta record, August 28, 1949 of 113.79 mph.

Below-A typical Evans Equipped Ford flathead engine at El Mirage Dry Lake in 1948.

Paul Schiefer's (Scheifer Flywheels) beautiful "T" lakes roadster up from San Diego. Paul's cars were not only beautiful but they hauled!

Stu Hilborn's streamliner at speed, El Mirage Dry Lake, 1947.

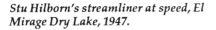

Paul Scheifer's "C" class roadster. This San Diego entry turned 148.02 mph one way. SCTA El Mirage, 1948. Harmon/Collins cam.

Wes Cooper and Bob Hays built this high-revving 4-barrel lakes roadster. Its 214 cubic inch engine turning 5800 rpm flashed through the SCTA traps at 142.18 mph in 1949. Fargo head, Kong ignition, Windfield cam.

Below-The Burke/Francisco tank kicks up lake dust on its way to trip the SCTA lights. First tank to go over 150 mph (151.085) in 1947. Dry weight of car was 1289 pounds.

Left-"Tipping the can" to a flathead-powered belly tank lakester. El Mirage Dry Lakes, 1947-48.

Below-A typical post-war rear-engined belly tank at El Mirage Dry Lake in 1947.

The Blair Speed Shop boys taking a break at a 1947 lakes meet. Uncle Donald was running his blown modified "Goat" at this meet.

Manny Ayulo taking it easy in old #44 track roadster. This car was used by MGM as a camera car to film the racing picture "To Please A Lady", starring Clark Gable and Barbara Stanwick.

Below-Jack McGrath, also a consistent front row qualifier at Indy in the '50s, is pictured here with his lakes and street '32 roadster converted to roundy-round racing. Carrell Speedway, Gardena, California, 1946.

Jack McGrath #1 on the pole. Troy Ruttman #24 (the Elco Twin Special) gets set for the trophy dash at Carrell Speedway in Gardena, California in 1947. Both later became Indy 500 stars.

Below-Here is SCTA's fastest roadster of 1948 (148.27 mph) set up to go oval track racing against CRA's best. Regg Schlemmer is owner/builder.

A typical CRA (California Roadster Association) track car that ran on the Carrell Speedway in the late '40s. CRA also ran at Bonelli Stadium, Saugus, California and at the Huntington Beach Speedway in Huntington Beach, California.

18

An Evans equipped '32 Vickey comes off the starting line at an early post-war Russetta meet, El Mirage Dry Lake.

Below-Custom southern California roadster with chopped windshield, trick grille (La-Salle?). Not too shabby for 1936!

John Lightfoot's "T"-bodied "B" roadster. 1938 Chevy engine with 232 cubic inches, Chevy head, special manifold, three Linkert carburetors, Harmon cam. Time: 115.08 mph. SCTA Lancers club member.

Below- Spalding Zephyr dual-coil ignition. Designed and built by Tom Spalding while a freshman in high school.

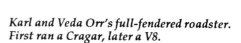

Karl and Veda Orr's full-fendered roadster. First ran a Cragar, later a V8.

Above-1929 roadster on '32 rails sets sail for the timing lights at a 1948 SCTA El Mirage meet. Check those "wind" tires on the rear.

A super smooth '29 roadster on '32 rails waits in line at a 1949 SCTA meet. This "C" roadster belongs to a "Hornets" SCTA club member.

Johnny Hartman's GMC (Wayne Head) powered lakes/track roadster. Full torsion bar suspension.

T. Medley, "Stroker" himself, getting his usual sunburn and photographs at a 1947-48 lakes meet.

Above-Start of a CRA "quick heat" at Gardena 1947-48. Manny Ayulo's #44 on the pole. Many of these cars also ran the lakes. Ayulo drove Indy cars in the '50s.

Darrell "Tim" Timmerman, early Blair Speed Shop engine builder, tries not to lose an arm while working on Manny Ayulo's #44 track roadster.

Don Blair tends his booth in the first hot rod show sponsored by SCTA and held at the national guard armory in Los Angeles from January 21-30, 1949.

Pat Flaherty, 1956 Indy winner, shown here in 1947-48 in Bob Estes beautiful track roadster at Gardena, California.

Ford V8-powered modified gets tender loving care from its owner at this pre-war lakes meet.

Bob Rufi's record-holding Chevrolet-powered streamliner. 140+ mph. Note the pants on the rear wheels. This was flying for the pre-war period.

An unidentified tail job, Muroc Dry Lake, 1939. Looks like an ex-Ascot track job.

A quick pit stop for this '34 flathead coupe in the Western Service Motel, where all the racers stayed (if they could get a room). Located in beautiful downtown Wendover. Speed Week, 1951.

Sandy Belond in his '32 roadster, before the war (1942). Sandy pioneered the exhaust header business and in the mid '50s sponsored several Indianapolis cars. The car driven to victory by Sam Hanks in 1957 was known as the Belond "Equa-Flo" Special.

Don Blair's blown modified known as "The Goat" ran 135 mph right after the war. Don has been a member of the L.A. Gophers and Pasadena Roadster club. His famous Blair's Speed Shop is still going strong ... with a new owner.

Old "57", Don Blair's track roadster ran a 124.88 mph run at a 1947 Russetta timing meet. Merc engine was 1/4 stroker by 3-5/16 running on straight gas. Car was very successful in southern California and was later sold to Andy Granatelli.

Right-A '32 hiboy roadster, complete with whitewalls, set sail down the dry El Mirage lake bed at a 1947 SCTA meet.

Below-Back in the good old days, before WWII when crash helmets were soft leather and the cars a lot less sophisticated than today.

SCTA meets could not be run without assigned club duties. As this '32 roadster heads down the course, the Miller's Club patrol car keeps the spectators away from the starting area.

The Pomona Valley Timing Association's own streamlined dragster, before paint, back in 1954. This beautiful dragster was featured in the June issue of Hot Rod Magazine, with a cut-away drawing by Rex Burnett. Dawson Hadley and Ed Vogel designed and built most of the car. PVTA members, lead by Manny Vallejo, also put in countless hours of work. Powered by a Hilborn injected Chrysler V8 running a Potvin cam and H&C magneto, the dragster turned 134.32 mph at the 1954 Southern California Championship meet.

Above-Superchargers similar to the one pictured here were starting to appear on all types of flathead V8-powered cars in the early '50s. Four carburetors feed this little beauty.

Right-As nice looking a rear-engine modified roadster as you would want to see was the Quincy Automotive D class Bonneville car. This was a top competitor at the early Bonneville Nationals.

One of the many beautifully constructed Bonneville streamliners that came to the salt in the early '50s. These boys had the right idea, bring your own shade!

George Cerney's stock-bodied '32 tudor with a 3-inch top chop drove the boys mad at Santa Ana dragstrip during the '50s, where he ran 123.45 mph on gas. The engine is a Cadillac with dual 4-throat carburetors. This is the same engine that smoked his 1953 Olds passenger car through the Bonneville lights at 135 mph. The addition of an Isky cam to the engine jumped the '32 tudor 1/4-mile speed from 117 mph to 123 mph.

Here's a one-of-a-kind roadster that was on hand at Santa Ana dragstrip one Sunday in the early '50s. The parking area was filled with most any kind of car imaginable.

This '29 roadster was typical of roadsters set up for quarter-mile action during the early days of drag racing. This car was on hand for an early NHRA Pomona drag meet.

An early dragster seen at Pomona dragstrip in the '50s. Note the push bar set-up and fuel pressure pump. Crude by today's standards, but it got the job done.

A good looking modified "D" roadster on the salt during the 1954 Speed Week. Must be a new car, check the paper plate.

Below-T. Medley's '36 convertible. The top was built under a street light by Stroker in 1946 while living in Portland. Mr. Flemming, Portland Top, gave guidance and did the final sewing, resulting in Tom going to work in the auto trim business.

This sneaky "C" class modified roadster gets a push start down the long black line during SCTA's Speed Week in 1954.

Ollie Morris' early '50s rear-engine dragster. The hand-formed all aluminum body was constructed of .052 half-hard material. Total car weight was 1550 lbs. Horsepower was furnished by a 275 cu.in. '46 Merc engine with a 4-inch stroke and Potvin cam, Edelbrock heads and manifold. At the 1954 Pacific Southwest Regional drags, held at the Paradise Mesa, California strip, Ollie's little rear-engine hummer recorded a 1/4-mile speed of 133.57 mph. The car's best was 140 mph. It lost to the Bean Bandits dragster in a run-off.

A Chrysler hemi V8 replaced the mighty flatmotor in Ollie Morris' rear-engine dragster for a try on the Bonneville salt. Ollie and friend burn the midnight oil in a garage in Wendover, Utah during an early '50s Bonneville Nationals meet.

It's Smoke City as a '29 roadster streaks down the Pomona dragstrip during one of the early '50s NHRA meets.

Above-A typical flat V8, set up for drag racing during the early '50s. No radiator was used, just the water in the block and heads were used for cooling.

Upper right-The early days of drag racing was the fun time of the sport. Cars were built with little money and everyone had their own idea what would go the quickest down the 1/4 mile course. This crew had their version on hand at an early Pomona, California meet.

Right-An early NSRA drag meet at the Pomona strip. Every body style, from coupes to dragsters, were on hand to take their shot at the 1/4-mile lights.

Could this have been the first rear-engined dragster? I'm sure it wasn't, but it shows that even in the early '50s the boys were trying new ideas. This car showed up at an early Pomona meet.

Tom Beatty's room at the Western Motel was easy to find ... just look for the stack of flathead blocks, portable "A" frame and his '40 Ford panel delivery — the one with the big stroker flathead for power. He surprised many a '54 Caddy by blowing past them on the highway with his race car in tow, and the panel loaded down with flathead engines.

As Tom Beatty's Weiand-sponsored tank ran supercharged flatmotors, he naturally blew his share, thus the many extra blocks. If he could get down super quick and qualify for a record, great. If the engine blew, no sweat .... dial in another.

This '34 3-window coupe shows a Blair Speed Shop sticker on the windshield, however the owner is unidentified. Water tank is in the rear. Two large hoses carry the coolant water to and from the engine. Note the small water hose outlets in the heads.

Whenever Tom Beatty would go into his flathead juggling act, he was bound to draw a crowd. It's not every day you get to see one of Bonneville's top speed kings doing his engine magic.

This long Sharp-equipped belly tank layout looks to be running two engines for power.

Good looking fully enclosed streamliner sponsored by Belond Equa-Flow Exhaust Systems. Bonneville, 1954.

Another one of the neat street roadsters that drove to the '53 Bonneville event. Even though in primer, its full belly pan and 2-piece windshield turned some heads.

Here it is, Wendover's finest ... the Western Motel. The largest in town in the early '50s. The parking area at night was an all-night garage. Lots of six packs and bench racing. Fun, fun, fun!

Don Clark of C.T. Automotive, hard at work on an Ardun-powered tank in the Western Motel parking area during the 1954 SCTA salt bash.

Close-up of the C.T. 284 cu.in. Ardun overhead Merc engine. Bore: 3-5/16", stroke: 4-1/8". A sliding-valve, constant-flow fuel injector designed and built by Don Clark and Clem Tebow. This engine ran a two-way average of 162.162 mph in a '32 hiboy roadster. Chet Herbert roller tappet cam was used.

This Hilborn injected Ardun-powered '29 roadster gets some serious wrench time in the motel parking lot.

This very slippery modified '34 Ford coupe runs a "C" class DeSoto hemi V8 engine. Beautiful paint!

Not all roadsters on the salt were competition cars. Here's a fine Edelbrock-equipped '27 "T" roadster that drove out to spectate. Lots of chrome ... and salt!

The Western Motel turn around parking area was like a car show during Speed Week. This very clean '29 roadster pulled in after being flat towed all the way to Wendover.

Ak Miller, pioneer Bonneville racer, gets ready for a pass through the lights in his 320+ cu.in. Olds-powered modified roadster. Engine featured homemade injectors, regulated from the cockpit. Car ran 168 mph at the 1953 Speed Week event.

Ak Miller's 1954 Bonneville entry shows slight outward modifications. Note air box over engine and needle nose addition. This car collected 3 records in one day. Not an easy task considering the time requirement. The records were: "A" class — 142 mph with a 136 cu.in. Ford V8 60; "B" class — 162 mph; "C" class — 176 mph with a 274 cu.in. flathead. This chassis featured independent suspension all the way around. Those are not Moon discs. Ak spun these for himself and Dean Moon borrowed the tooling and sold them commercially as Moon discs.

The Summers Brothers and Johnson "E" class modified roadster waits its turn for a trip down the salt. Note air box over engine area and fresh air scoop alongside driver.

In the early days of Bonneville, you had better bring along tools and equipment to fix anything that might break on your car. This group brought along half of their garage and it pays off by giving a helping hand to a hot rodder in need of some welding.

This '34 Ford "C" coupe owner checks one of the heads off his Ford flathead V8 powerplant. Everywhere you looked in those days, flathead engines were being worked on. The girlfriend or wife in the truck is getting some zzzz's.

This is what you call a full house. A blown hemi Chrysler shoehorned into what looks to be a Ford pickup truck. Impressive!

The Waters and Murry '29 "C" class roadster rolls off the trailer for another day on the salt. A very pretty roadster.

A Hilborn fuel injected hemi marine Chrysler engine, complete with magneto, ready to pump out some heavy horsepower on the salt.

This slippery looking streamliner, getting some between-run wrench action is powered by two Chrysler hemi engines. The two rear drive tires are 18" Indianapolis Speedway tires.

A Canadian roadster heads out to the salt from downtown Wendover. Not much has changed since this early '50s picture.

Motorcycle 'liners also ran at Bonneville. Here "C.B." Clausen's cigar-shaped creation gets lined up on the rollers, ready for a start.

The starter bike gets the rollers humming and this, in turn, starts the streamliner's engine. When the engine has cleaned out, the 'liner is pushed off the rollers and off it goes down the course.

No, that object on top of the Sparks and Bonney '32 coupe is not a new style roll bar. The chopped top has been raised up to stock height with cardboard and masking tape so as to be legal in another class. Starter Bob Higbee checks it out.

In the early '50s, due to Hot Rod Magazine's coverage, cars came from all parts of the U.S. This Bonneville hopeful towed the car all the way from Ohio to run on the world famous salt. Who cares about a record, just tune 'em up and run. That's the fun of it all.

With the salt in perfect condition for this mid-'50s Speed Week, this "C" class modified roadster gets a push start to test the salt.

Lansing, Michigan is a long haul from the Bonneville salt, but this "D" class sedan made the trip and doesn't mind the wait in line to make a pass.

Bill Davis gets the Ardun-powered tank ready for the salt in the Western Motel parking lot in downtown Wendover, Utah. More engine changes and chassis work took place here than in most big city garages.

A typical Bonneville car running in the "C" roadster class. Cars in this class, running 296 cu. in. flatmotors, ran 160 mph. Hernandez & Likes, L.A., turned 160.142 mph in this class at the 1951 Bonneville meet in their hiboy '32 roadster.

Beautiful downtown Wendover, Utah in the '50s. Picture is shot looking out the road leading to the salt. On the left is the mighty Texaco garage where out in back many engine swaps took place. A little farther down is the Western Cafe and Motel where all the hot shoe racers stayed. Oh yeah! At the early meets, you stayed wherever you could find a room. Their weren't many. Many of the guys stayed in the Air Force barracks or camped out.

Bob Pierson gives Wally Parks a quick look at the full Edelbrock engine that powered the Pierson Brothers car to a 1950 Russetta "D" coupe record — 142.98 mph.

The third Russetta meet of the 1950 season saw the Callahan & Papworth chopped sedan tied for the meet's fastest speed — 139.75 mph.

Dean Moon of Moon eyeball fame, mixes fuel at '50s Bonneville meet. Dean ran cars at the lakes and the salt for years, and was a Bonneville regular.

The Perry Boys '29 "B" class roadster gets a push start down the rock-hard Bonneville salt. A very sharp looking salt roadster.

A '39 Ford "B" coupe, complete with Speedway tires and Moon discs, gets ready for a run down the salt.

This beautiful "C" class belly tank, owned and driven by Tom Beatty, runs a blown flathead engine and was a regular at Bonneville for years. Tom went through flathead engines by the truckload during a week at Wendover. He went like gangbusters while he was running.

Don Francisco, long time lakes and race car mechanic and former tech editor for Hot Rod Magazine, checks the action at an early Pomona Drag Strip event.

Jack McGrath, early '50s Indy driver of some note, poses for a quick photo after picking up a "fast time" trophy with his '32 roadster at an early dry lakes meet.

Post-war track roadster. This good looking '27 roadster displays neat craftsmanship, complete with roll bar and race car nose.

Left-Otto Crocker, chief timer for the SCTA, doing his thing with his Crocker timing system. Jim Lindsley, long time SCTA member assists.

Below-Here's an unusual 1947 roadster set-up, a 1938 LaSalle engine, ported and relieved, Winfield cam and milled heads. '32 roadster body is channeled. Car turned 118.83 mph on the dry lake bed, representing the Pasadena Roadster Club.

A member of the SCTA Roadrunners Club, Bill Niekamp built this exceptional '29 roadster. Frame rails are '29 Essex. Car was built for both street and lakes and won the 1950 Oakland Roadster Show's top award: America's Most Beautiful Roadster.

Chet Herbert Cams twin-engine radical streamliner "Beast 5" at the 1954 Bonneville Speed Week event. Leroy Newmeyer driver, Chet Herbert builder and owner.

Below-The Cagle/Fugatt "C" modified roadster waits in line at an early '50s Bonneville meet. Note the Indy 500 tires all around.

Above-A later version of the Chet Herbert streamliner, this time with 3 engines and the driver riding slingshot ala Mickey Thompson.

Left-The Lee Chapel streamliner ran many of the early Bonneville meets. Engine was fitted with Tornado V8 OHV heads. Lee Chapel started his first speed shop in L.A. in 1930, and later moved to Oakland.

Left-The Chrisman Brothers & Duncan dynamite Bonneville modified '30 coupe was without a doubt one of the wildest looking cars at the 1954 Bonneville Speed Week. It not only was a looker, but it could haul! How about "B" class 241 cu. in. Dodge - 186 mph. "C" class 276 cu. in. DeSoto, 187 mph. The next year, a Tony Cabana "D" class Chrysler powered the slippery Chrisman coupe with Art driving, at 96 mph plus. Not too shabby!

Above-Here the Chrisman crew slides the body back on the chassis after a quick engine change in downtown Wendover. Art's brother and dad were on the crew.

Body back in place, final bolt-up is being done prior to returning to the salt to go for another record. The sneaky nose was built from two '40 Ford deluxe hoods.

Art and Lloyd Chrisman built the car in approximately one year. Note how everything is designed for ease of engine change.

This is what the mighty 267 cu.in. "D" class DeSoto engine looked like just prior to installation. A Hilborn injector system and Vertex mag handled the fuel and spark chores. Engines were built for Harry Duncan by Tony Cabana.

Art and Lloyd Chrisman brought this coupe to the salt for the first time in 1953. They ran 157 mph with an Ardun-equipped flathead and 163 mph with a "C" class flatmotor on 50% nitro. Art did the driving.

Jim Lindsley, long time member of SCTA is pictured here in 1947 in his homemade "B" class streamliner which turned 132.93 mph. Jim is still active, running the salt every year.

This unique '25 "T" roadster built by Frank Palmer in 1934 won the 1949 Pasadena Roadster Club reliability run's best appearing car trophy. Runs a V8 engine. Car now owned by Ray Bowels.

Above left-Typical SCTA starting line scene at El Mirage dry lake in 1949. Note the starting line lights. Lights were made and installed by electrician Jim Lindsley and SCTA member.

Above-Ray Brown's rear-engine '27 "T" class "A" modified roadster when it was first built. Photo was taken at an SCTA meet in 1948.

Left-Ray Brown's refined V8 60 rear-engine roadster turned 134.73 mph at the June 1949 SCTA meet. The 1938 Ford V8 60 engine ran Evans heads and manifold, Harmon-Collins cam and Kong ignition. Car weighs 1500 pounds.

Right-This classic '32 street and lakes roadster turned 137.40 mph on pump gas, SCTA timed. The 258 cu.in. '42 Merc engine ran Edelbrock heads and manifold. Harmon-Collins cam and Potvin ignition. Owned by Dick Price, San Berdoo Roadster Club.

Below-Vic Edelbrock Sr., founder of Edelbrock Equipment Company, and Wally Parks founder of NHRA, looking over an early '50s Edelbrock-equipped engine.

Below right-Bill Likes, a top runner at the lakes in the early '50s, turned 137 mph in his '32 class "B" roadster on June 10, 1951. Bill ran all Edelbrock goodies.

Clem Tebow adjusts the carburetion on his mighty Ardun-equipped Ford flathead engine that provided the ponies for the very successful track car. This engine, with injectors, ran 164 mph one way, posting a two-way average of 162 mph in a hiboy '32 roadster at Bonneville in 1957.

Bob McGee's beautiful '32 roadster as it looked in 1948. This car was later purchased by Dick Scritchfield, long time L.A. Roadster Club member, and has kept it on the road to the present time.

Chopped '32 Ford tudor pictured in the Pomona Drag Strip parking lot, early 1950s. Note the full louvered hood.

A super-low, channeled '32 "C" class roadster waiting in line to make a run at a 1947 SCTA El Mirage meet.

A scene duplicated many times during the 1951 lakes season. Cars line up 3 abreast waiting to make a run. El Mirage dry lake, California.

Mickey Thompson at the controls of his super-fast #555 streamliner gets a fast shove from his pit crew at Bonneville Speed Week.

The Yeager & Shugart '36 Ford 3-window coupe owner takes a quick look-see into the "C" class engine room while waiting in line during an early '50s Bonneville meet

A close-up look at an injected Chrysler-powered '29 Bonneville roadster. Note the engine setback and Howard front drive unit that handles the ignition and injector pump. Bonneville, early '50s.

A typical port and relieve job on a 59A flathead block. This job was done by old "Dad" Taylor at Blair's Speed Shop in Pasadena. California in 1948.

Tom Medley's '49 Ford convertible with an Oldsmobile 88 Rocket engine and Hydromatic transmission. Installation was done by Hot Rod Magazine tech editor Don Francisco in the early '50s. A real fun sleeper!

Jack McMillan, Portland, Oregon bodyman par-excellance customized his '39
Ford convert to resemble a roadster. Windshield was chopped, special Carson-type
padded top, running boards removed and
license plate recessed. A really tasty piece
for 1946.

Dave Mitchell's
bright red '29
Model A pickup
was a great
example of con-
struction excel-
lence. Dave's little
pickup was second
in the balloting for
best appearing car
of the '49 P.R.C.
Reliability Run.
Originally built
with a Ford
flathead, it later
ran an Olds OHV
V8.

Here's what a Pacific Northwest roadster top looked like in 1946 in Portland, Oregon where it's been known to rain a little. Note the neat watertight side curtains and, of course, dual windshield wipers. The semi-padded top, complete with headliner, was built by Mr. Fleming of Portland Top Company.

The Stu Hilborn streamliner gets a plug change at Muroc dry lake prior to WWII.

One of Veda and Karl Orr's roadsters that they ran prior to the war. Photo was taken at a Western Timing meet. The car turned 127.17 mph.

As told by Kong Jackson

Ed Winfield was born October 4, 1901 in La Canada, California. When Ed was 4 or 4 1/2 his dad died, and he was telling me how the old horse and buggy pulled up to the house and took his dad away. His dad had been sick quite a bit. He never knew anything about his dad except he came from Chicago. His mother came from Norway. She was a house servant. She worked in the homes of rich people and raised her two kids on her own.

Ed finished 8 years of schooling, then he went to work for the YMCA school in Los Angeles as a parts boy. He rode bicycles all over town picking up parts. He told them one time he was going to quit and go back to La Canada and get a job. The teacher told him "Ed, just before you quit, let me know and we'll run you through the school."

They had an electrical and mechanical guy that was really super. They taught the basics all the way through, so Ed went through the school. He said the guys were geniuses...really smart guys. So, he learned from them, and he got to meet all the garage owners in L.A., from riding around on his bike. So he was familiar with them when he went into business.

Then, he came back to La Canada and got a job at the Flintridge garage. He worked there quite awhile, doing whatever they wanted him to do. He read every book he could get in the country for all the different cars, so whenever they had a real problem, they'd give it to Ed. He was just a kid, but he'd go tune it up and make it work.

Ed had a friend who was running a race car, an old T. One Sunday, they were working on the car, and somebody came down and said, "Ed, the boss wants you back up at the garage right now to go to work." Ed said he was working on his friend's car. The guy said, "I don't care, you got to come up there." So Ed just quit.

His mother worked for Senator Flint. That's where the town Flintridge came from. Anyway, his mother worked for Mrs. Flint and a couple of other rich ladies. Since Ed was out of work, his mother asked the Senator if they could get Ed a job. They got him a job at Cadillac. He worked there for a long time, then he moved up to North Grand to an independent garage. He worked there for a long time, and then he finally went into business on his own and moved down to Glendale.

He opened up a little garage and did engine stuff. Ed was building some carburetors, and he did a few cams by hand on his old hand grinder.

TOM: When did Ed get into racing?

KONG: He was running his T's, beating those Millers. One time, a driver took that T flathead race car and ran a lap on the board speedway at 132 miles an hour. Another time, he finished a 100 mile race in Inglewood, at the old dirt track. A hundred miles open in a Model T, and it was still running fine when he finished. Imagine that!

He got married in about 1925 or '26 and he quit racing. Ed met his future wife one day while she was walking down the street going to visit some relatives. Along came Ed in his little T roadster. There was a detour in the street. They had to stop and he got to talking to her, and ended up marrying her. So, roadsters were good pickup machines, even then.

Later on, his wife's health got bad, so they decided to move to San Francisco to get away from the smog. They stayed there for a while, but the smog started getting bad there. One weekend they drove over to

Las Vegas and found a house. Ed had a shop built in the back, moved all his equipment there, and started grinding cams. Semi-retired, he ground up until about '70.

Harmon told me one time, "Of all the guys that grind cams, there was only one Winfield. He was above everybody else."

TOM: He must have ground cams for all the race car guys.

KONG: Everybody that really went, like all the B flatheads. All the good engines, up until the time he quit. His stuff was accurate. You could pick up one of his cams, and mic the heel and they were all within a .001. On a valve cam you can be rough, as long as it opens somewhere near what you want. But, an ignition cam, there's no tolerance. You have to be dead on. If one lobe is two or three thousandths different the timing goes bad.

Even before the war, he was grinding all the good ones. Offy sent all the cams to Ed. He was grinding stuff for us on the side. We got some Cragar cams, and some Riley cams right up to the very end. He ground

What the well-dressed race driver wore in 1924. Here's Ed Winfield, complete with vest, tie and good pair of goggles. Photo was taken at Ascot Speedway in Los Angeles.

my ignition cams. The last thing he ground on his grinder were some Model A cam blanks left over. He ground all those, about 30 of them, and he said, "Here...you might as well take these." Those were the last Winfield cams, and we've still got them.

He got that big automatic grinder from Landis right after the war. Grind a complete master cam, put it into the machine and press the button. It will grind one cam lob, then move on to the next one. When he got that going, he figured he could grind a cam for about $3 labor. He was selling

them out the door by the hundreds. Edelbrock, everybody was selling them.

In '56, he had boxes of brand new cores. He paid $6 and something for wholesale. The wholesale at Ford was up to about $17. So he called up Meyer-Welch, the engine rebuilding place, and asked them if they would like to buy some stock cams. They said no.

So, we were sitting there one day, and he said, "Do you think we could sell some cams cheap?"

I said, "I don't know why not."

He had about 700 brand new stock cams, and there were a few 3/4 ground up that nobody would buy. So we ran a 3-inch ad in Hot Rod Magazine. It said, "Winfield cams. 50-70% off." The highest price was $20 down to $12. Even before the ad came out, a bunch of guys started calling, "What's this Kong doing selling cams so cheap?"

So, we started selling 30 or 40 a day. The UPS would come to my house, and we'd load that guy up and we were shipping them all over the country. For three months we ran the ad, and we sold completely out. We sold all the cams, and for a year I was getting orders for cams. I was getting $2 apiece for each cam. He had paid the initial cost, plus labor. So, he was making $4 to $8 a cam. If we had those today...oh, man...$100 - $200 easy!

If someone knocked on the door of his shop, he'd open the door and if you talked right or if he knew you, he'd open the door and let you in the lobby. The average guy could get in the lobby, but that's all. If you were a friend, or he liked you, he'd take you into the shop. There weren't very many guys that got into the shop. I got along with him, from the first. But if you asked him something, you didn't interrupt him. Pay attention.

TOM: How old was he, when he passed away?

KONG: He was born in 1901, and he died April 15, 1982. He would have been 81, October 4 that same year. During his lifetime, Winfield's inventions, his patents, covered the first fuel injection into an induction system. The Bendix/Stromberg carburetor during WWII had a little diaphragm pump down in the face of the impeller. The carburetor was all pressure differential. It would inject the fuel into the face of the impeller. That was all Ed's patent. And the constant flow fuel injection that's used in aircraft and everything else today, was Ed's patent. His patent ran out in '56, and Chevrolet came out with their version of it the next year.

In 1940, Hilborn and a guy named Miller who worked for him, went over to Ed's, and Ed showed him all the blueprints...explained how it worked. Ed's unit had a barometric control, like they run on aircraft; real fuel control. All they used was a pump, a nozzle, and a restriction, which most of them run today. Ed's patent, which is on file, covers all that basic stuff. He was the first. He checked with GM and a bunch of people; they weren't interested.

TOM: What amazed me was how fast the the 4-cylinders would run with the Winfield flathead.

KONG: They were 6:1 compression, when they were all running at Ascot, and the B's were running down there in '35 or '36. They came out with a new rule. You could run 200 cid, and 7:1. So, Ed says, "We'll make a head."

So, he sketched up a head on a couple pieces of paper, and gave it to a pattern maker in L.A., and for a couple of hundred dollars, he made a pattern. It was a poor, pine pattern. You had to set the combustion chamber core separate. Anyway, they made the head, put it on and they dominated. They got protested so they pulled it apart, and checked the compression. Rex Mays drove that car, and they were champions in '36.

TOM: Did Bob Rufi run a Winfield cam?

KONG: Oh, yes. He had Winfield carburetor parts on his adapter side deal. All those guys that went fast, they all went to Winfield, and talked to him.

TOM: That engine that Rufi ran was a Chevy 4, with an Olds 3-port head?

KONG: There was a 3-port Olds, and then there was a Tornado head, that old Chapple. It was similar, but the porting was a little different. Everybody figured it was a 3-port, but Cooper looked at it and figured it was a Tornado-type head.

And like Ernie McAfee, he ran 132 with a flathead and a little tin body. That thing had a 6:1, and he started it with the crank...one carburetor. He'd put his hand over the carburetor to choke it, pull the crank up...and it would go.

They ran flatheads at the track, too. And the flatheads would actually pick the overheads up at the end of the straight-aways. The overheads would get up to a point, and the flatheads would keep on pulling.

There was a guy in Glendale who had a little T roadster. Ed built him an engine for it. One day, the guy drives up to Oakland in his T. He was running a race car, and blew the engine. So they took the engine out of the T roadster, put it in the race car and qualified at 90 mph. Finished the race, took it out, put it in the roadster, and drove it home. Ed's stuff was tops.

TOM: What about the old car runs to Las Vegas in recent years to visit Ed?

KONG: We started in 1976. We'd have about 25 cars; roadsters, sedans, etc. Most all were 4-cylinder Fords. We would drive to Vegas and spend the weekend visiting Ed. It was a ball. We usually had 30 to 50 guys making the trip. We continued until 1981.

Ed passed away April 15th, 1982. Thus ended the life of a man whose contributions will forever be etched on the pages of hot rod history.

Not all the racers were as successful as Ed Winfield, as can be seen in this early photo of the #6 Redlands Special that was destroyed after a trip through the fence.

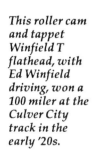

This roller cam and tappet Winfield T flathead, with Ed Winfield driving, won a 100 miler at the Culver City track in the early '20s.

Ascot Speedway in Los Angeles in the early '20s. Ed Winfield is in the #1 car on the side. The track became so dusty at times the boys could hardly see. Great racing, however.

The Winfield T flathead #1 charges to the lead on the outside. Ed is in his usual racing cap and goggles. Ascot Speedway, L.A.

Ed Winfield being congratulated by a AAA official on winning the helmet dash at Ascot Speedway, 1926. Johnny Famalaro, Bud Winfield and crew member look on.

Racing has always been popular in California. Here a field of early racers prepare to get off and running right after WWI. Notice no grandstands and no condominiums on the hills! Those were the days.

Ed Winfield lays the screwdriver to one of his carburetors on the Gilmore Red Lion Special at Legion Ascot Speedway in the 1930s.

Ed Winfield (center with goggles around neck) and crew with Ed's first car at Hanford, California July 4th, 1921. A Model T flathead of course. Ed drove the car to the track.

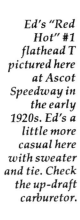

Ed's "Red Hot" #1 flathead T pictured here at Ascot Speedway in the early 1920s. Ed's a little more casual here with sweater and tie. Check the up-draft carburetor.

To the victor go the spoils. Ed Winfield displays the trophy for winning a 100 mile race in 1926. Picture taken at 1419 Pico Blvd., Los Angeles, California.

Ed Winfield as a boy racer displays the latest in dirt track racing head gear. Ed's ever present goggles complete his racing outfit. Heck, that's all you needed besides a heavy foot! Ascot Speedway, 1920s.

The ever present goggles and tie seemed to be the trademark of the young Ed Winfield, whose flathead T was tearing 'em up at Ascot Speedway in the '20s.

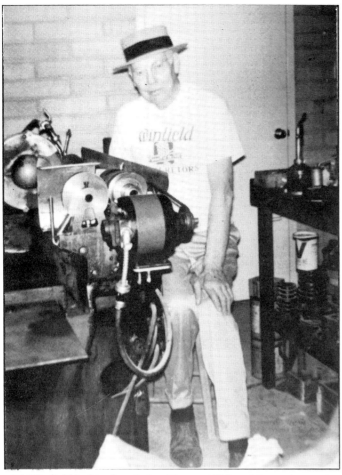

Ed Winfield in his shop in Las Vegas still knocking out cams in 1972. When this photo was taken, Ed was 70 years old and still going strong.

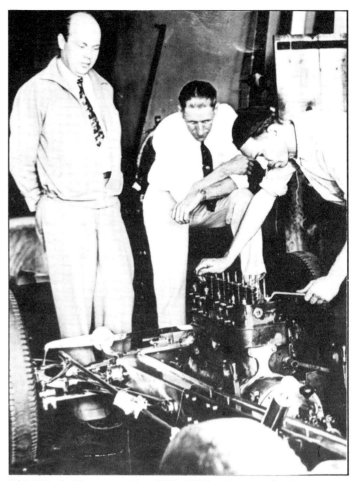

This Winfield set-up, a 7 to 1 Winfield rocker arm head on an A block driven by Rex Mays was protested by the 2-cam Miller boys for being illegal. Actually, the engine was only 183 cu.in. running against 200 cu.in. max engines. (L to R) Ed Winfield, Paul Frome.

Ed Winfield "hauling the mail" in his famous #1 Winfield T flathead. Running a special billet 2-up/2-down crankshaft, this set-up with Ed driving in 1926-'27 was a terror on the dirt. Soon after this, Ed tried married life and from then on, no more racing.

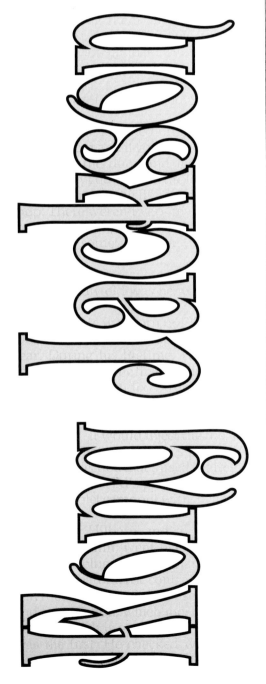

Early Lakes

TOM: When's the first time you went to the lakes?

KONG: I went in '37 with my roadster, but we didn't run. We got to Muroc too late for the first runs. A guy there said, "If you wanna run, come back as soon as we finish our run-off races. But, we didn't wait. Then in '38, I was stationed right there in the Mojave. When I came home, I joined the Sidewinders and started runnin' in '39.

The Road Runners, Ninety Mile an Hour, the Sidewinders and the throttlers were the four original clubs. They got together and had a few meetings, just before the end of '37. In the first month of '38, they incorporated into the SCTA. Before that, guys were getting killed at the lakes, and running into each other. No organization, or nuthin'.

TOM: Who was running the clocks originally?

KONG: The Purdy Brothers. And then there was the Russetta bunch and the Mojave Timing. Russetta got started in '40 and '41. Mojave Timing was running the lakes in '41. Everybody recognized the SCTA as the premier group.

Once I got active, I started running all the time from '39 on. I got elected to the board in '39. I was at an Association meeting one night, representing our club, and the president called me up one night and said, "I've got a bunch of guys who would like to see you on the board." So they put me on the board.

Mel Layton was running the start and we were helping. Then in '41 we took over. We had the whole starting line, the tech committee and in general the whole starting part of the lakes. After the war, we had the same duties, except we organized a timing stand, and put women on it. It kept the wives and girlfriends active. They weren't sitting and waiting in the car or at home, they were up there and they were the last word! Nobody got by them. They did an excellent job, therefore our lakes meets ran very efficiently. The tech committee worked well. Every guy who had a car, had a couple of buddies helping him. So, we were never short of help.

TOM: Weren't you up at Muroc the day the army threw you off the lake bed?

KONG: I sure was. In May '41 we had run one of the lake meets. The last one we ran was in July of '41. From then on we were running at Harper. We ran at Rosemond a few times, but it was a poor lake bed. The army took it over for bombing practice in '41.

We heard about the meet at Muroc in November. I loaded up my roadster and drove up and there were a lot of people. Man, everywhere you looked, just like an SCTA meet. We took the windshield and headlights off, and put 'em in a pile. In those days people didn't steal 'em. We put the tarp on, and got in line. I think we ran about 109 mph, but the wind was blowing 45 degrees across the course. In fact, it was blowing so hard on one of the runs I was blown entirely off the course. We made four or five runs, and we were just returning from the finish line, and here came all these army types. We saw 'em coming and we knew what they were, because the U.S. Army Air Corp was southeast of where we were running, and all the dust and dirt was blowing through their camp.

So, we pulled up to where we had stacked our headlights and stuff and started loading it all back into the car. We had just put the windshield back on the car, when here came a Jeep and out jumped these guys with bayonets. Man, we just split! But it was real funny, because in two months 90% of the guys on the lakes were in the service. Everybody I knew was gone.

You know that car of Abbott's and Sunshine's? Well, Sunshine had two Winfields on the log manifold he had made up, and he'd run alcohol at the lakes. When he got ready to go home, he'd drive it 'til it ran out of alcohol, and screw the needles in and put gas in it. He was coming in on that Palmdale road, at El Mirage, and Sunshine always drove full bore no matter where he was going. We'd all come in there at 80-90 mph. Anyway, he was coming in one Sunday in his roadster goin' about 90 mph. And this guy in a little single-engine plane dives on him. Wants to race. Sunshine sees him and sort of gets on it. Sunshine pulls the airplane and the guy dove on him and keeps diving on him, and Sunshine keeps pulling him. So, they get down to this

This very straight '32 hiboy street roadster ran a Ford flathead engine with 3/8" overbore, stock stroke, ORD manifold and Kong ignition. Ran 125 mph SCTA after the war.

intersection, and there was a dip there. If you hit it at about 30 mph, you could turn over. They were always having wrecks. Brown was doing about 100.

Well, he hit that dip, and went up in the air, and was flying wing with the airplane. When he landed he was in the ditch on the opposite side of the road. But Brown just stood on it, kept right on going down the dirt back onto the road. If there had been a car or anything there, they'd have all been dead. And if that airplane had gotten a little closer, he'd have knocked it out of the air. He must have been 30 feet up in the air. That would have been some headline: "A-V8 KNOCKS AIRPLANE OUT OF SKY"!

TOM: More guys crashed on the road gettin' to the lakes. Right after the war, Tim Timmerman and I were following a bunch of taillights. All of a sudden they were going this way and that, and all of a sudden the taillights disappeared. Then we saw some headlights pointed way up, and some guy just dumped his '36 roadster.

KONG: Well, they all thought they were racers! They'd go full bore on unknown ground. In '39 we were sitting in some little restaurant, and here comes some guy in a Chrysler Airflow. He stops and says, "Where's the lakes"?

The guys point that-a-way, and he takes off

— he was gonna race. About an hour later we went down the road, and there he was turned upside down in a big gully.

TOM: You built your first ignition after the war, the one that they were using on the flatheads?

KONG: In '41, I built up a couple of ignitions, but not as fancy as I wanted. During the war, I knew what I wanted to do, so, I made the patterns up for the ignitions. Bought the caps, rotors, points and bearings, and I started making ignitions. Edelbrock had his manifolds before the war, and he worked for a machine shop all during the war. So did Weiand. They were making manifolds during the war from surplus metal, I understand. Paul Schiefer from San Diego started making flywheels and clutches during this period.

Here's something about Paul Schiefer — a lot of guys might take credit for it, but Schiefer was the first guy to run cycle wheels on a roadster at the lakes. Everybody looked at 'em and shook their heads, but he had 'em first, and they worked.

TOM: What about Hartman's track car, with the torsion bars and all that stuff. Was that a piece of work, or what?

KONG: Oh, yeah that sucker handled. Hartman ran lakes and the track in '49 or '50. He ran 146 mph at the lakes. Cooper with his four-barrel ran 142 mph, and a V8 was third. If Cooper had had some decent tires, instead of those rotten knobbies, he'd have run 160 mph, 'cause he was flyin'.

TOM: Where did you meet Akmo, Tom McLaughlin?

KONG: When I got back from working for the government, I came home, got out my roadster and rebuilt the engine, and got it running on the street. About the first guy I ran into was Akmo, who came along and said, "Where's this Kong guy, I hear he's got a racer"?

So, the guys pointed over to me and he said, "You think you got a racer"?

I said, "No, it's just a V8."

About a month later, he pulls up beside me right in front of Hoover High School, in a '31 blue-green thing with a checker board grille. It was a flathead. So, man, we took off down the street. And we were only down the road about a half a block and there were some other cars coming, so I had to stop. He said, "Well, I beat 'cha!"

Then in '38 we went out on Glenoaks near Hansen Dam. There were two guys from Glendale named Vic and Mac who ran a 2-port Riley, a '29 stripped roadster at the lakes. They ran 99 something. One night in '39 they came up to where we hung out and said, "Hey, any of you guys wanna race"?

We set up a date for the next day. Akmo's car was there, and a guy named Rex who hung around with Akmo. We were all lined up on Glenoaks. There must have been 500 guys there. They were lined up on both sides of the road.

So we all three lined up, and when they said,"GO" we just took off, and they never saw us again. We beat 'em both. We beat that 2-port Riley, and when you can beat a 2-port Riley from a dead stop you have to run strong. He was pretty upset. Mine ran awful good there for a stocker. That was before I had the good Winfield or anything.

TOM: You know, Akmo was the world's greatest street racer, until he was all done.

KONG: You know, when you start thinking about all the wild things you did in those days, you kind of wonder how you ever made it. I'm still crazy as ever about Ford flathead engins. As you know I'm making special heavy-duty heads for the lakes and drag racers. Also still making ignitions. I've got a special flathead V8 engine that I plan to run this year at Bonneville in a 'liner. It should run 200 plus. So, I guess you never outlive your love for hot rods, no matter how old you get.

Starting line-up of roadsters on Harpers dry lake right after WWII.

Kong Jackson leans on his '32 roadster at Harpers dry lake in 1940. The shell and hood were borrowed from another '32 Ford before driving to the meet. Long known for his ignitions, Kong now makes super strong flathead V8 heads and manifolds for the serious competitor.

Kong himself, with the first dual coil, dual point ignition array he made after serving as an Air Force mechanic during WWII.

Freddie Huber, aboard Kong Jackson's super immaculate '32 roadster. Shown here at a 1941 Muroc lakes meet. The 21-stud V8 engine sports the first tall Weiand manifold.

One of the Sidewinders patrol cars, Fred Huber does his duty in his '32 3-window coupe. He ran this car at Russetta, and turned 98 mph with a stock mill and slingshot manifold.

Below-"Richie" Richards at speed on Muroc dry lake (where the Space Shuttle now lands) in 1937. Turned 104 mph with his Ford V8 flathead.

Above-This '29 roadster was driven from Los Angeles to Muroc dry lake bed where fenders and headlights were removed. Then the driver, known as "Moose" fired up his Cragar and was ready to go racing. The year was 1937, when things were much simpler!

Right-Warren Van Sickel's '32 roadster gets the once-over from Kong Jackson. Check out the welded-up 4-97 carburetor manifold. The year was 1940.

Below-A typical 1935 Ford 5-window coupe complete with skirts and chrome discs. Driver is unknown, but check the helmet and goggles! 1940 vintage.

Above-The Glendale Sidewinders boys park at 314 W. Colorado Blvd., prior to starting off to the Puente Time Trials in 1939.

Left-Kong Jackson, veteran dry lakes runner, is pictured here at Muroc dry lake, May 1941 in his sano '32 roadster. His 236 cu.in. Ford flathead engine, equipped with Jahns flat-top pistons, .090" overbore, Winfield super cam, filled and milled heads, tall Weiand manifold, and Kong ignition, turned 110 mph on gas!

1939 hitchhikers Kong and Carter clown it up a bit at the top of Cajon Pass on the way home from Harpers dry lake.

One of the first Weiand "tail" dual carb Ford V8 manifolds is shown here on Kong Jackson's '32 Roadster in the early '40s.

An early pre-war 4-carb manifold welded up to fit a Ford 21-stud V8 engine. Anything was tried to make 'em go faster. If you couldn't buy it, you had to make it.

Kong Jackson's flathead V8 engine equipped with the first Kong ignition, Meyer heads, Winfield cam and ORD manifold. This engine turned 125 mph on alky in Kong's '32 roadster in the early '40s.

The Glendale Sidewinders stop for a roadside break between Lancaster and Palmdale, California on the way back home from Muroc dry lake in 1938.

Kong Jackson's 1939 SCTA membership card. He is still active today. Currently manufacturing super strong competition heads, ignitions and manifolds for flathead Ford V8s.

MEMBERSHIP CARD—1939

This Is to Certify That

Charles Jackson

is a Member in Good Standing of the

Southern California Timing Association, Inc.
Los Angeles, Calif.

Date Issued *Feb. 6, 1939*

Edward M Adams
PRESIDENT

Art Tilton
SECRETARY

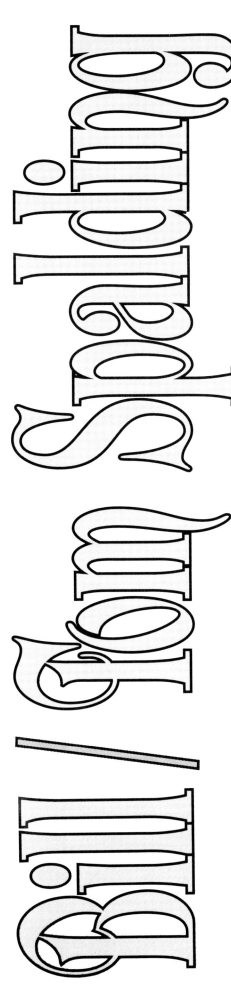

Bill / Tom Spalding

T. MEDLEY: When did you guys first go to the lakes?

TOM: We first went to the lakes in 1934, but had to settle for spectating since we didn't even have a driver's license at the time. But the sights, sounds and excitement of the lakes captured our attention, and it didn't take long to catch the bug to go racing ourselves.

T. MEDLEY: Tell me about the cars you ran.

TOM: The first car we ran at the lakes was a Model A touring car. Next came a flathead roadster, followed by a '38 modified flathead V8 with milled heads, a cam and our own homemade manifold. That car clocked speeds in excess of 120 mph. Next came a streamliner called the "Carpet Sweeper" which ran the same engine that was in the modified — but in this car it turned 138 mph. The fifth car was a '29 Ford roadster that bore #2 on its side and was equipped with Riley OHV heads. That was followed by a modified which ran the Riley OHV on a flathead block, and was assisted by a Mercedes blower.

We ran most every 4-cylinder conversion set-up available in the pre-war period; 2-port and 4-port Rileys, Crager, Miller-Schofield, Winfield, flathead, Dryer OHV.

T. MEDLEY: When did you build your first A-V8?

TOM: We built our first A-V8 in 1936 (Bob Stelling built one at the same time). The engine was purchased at a wrecking yard on Soto Street in Los Angeles, and a '33 X-member was used. These cars were the first A-V8s in southern California, along with Bill Johnson's a Pasadena hot rodder. Bob Stelling and I had the only roadsters. Bill's was a touring.

T. MEDLEY: How did you get into the igniton business?

TOM: It was the A-V8 that was responsible for getting into the ignition business. The V8 would cut out at about 4500 rpm, so I built the first dual-point/dual-coil ignition in the machine shop, while still a sophomore in high school. I purchased the dual-coil from Coberly Lincoln/Mercury in L.A. and fabricated the rest myself. I had the run of the high school machine shop for hot rod projects such as milling heads, cutting down rearends, etc.

My first ignition system ran great, and the engine would turn 5500 to 6000 rpm. The system caught on, and soon I was building them for other racers at the lakes. I ran this ignition on my modified and turned 120 mph.

T. MEDLEY: What about the streamliner?

TOM: When the streamliner was built, it had a 91" wheelbase and ran Essex rails. Because aluminum was too expensive, the skin was made of sheet steel. Without the body, the streamliner was a great drag car. We challenged all comers at our Orange Grove dragstrip (a measured and marked 1/4-mile strip) near our home in Glendora, California.

T. MEDLEY: Tell me about the famous $5 car.

TOM: I bought the '29 roadster for $5, which turned out to be a perfect deal. I sold the wheels for $5 and found 3 cents under the seat, so I made money on the deal! We ran the V8 block with a set of Riley OHV heads. I made a special welded-up dash, which was the first of its kind. The gas tank went in the back.

The blown modified was the last car we ran before the war (1941). Later, this car was purchased by Don Blair and was known as the "Goat" while running the lakes after the war.

T. MEDLEY: And then you got into track cars?

TOM: When the war broke out, I went in the Navy and became a career pilot. After the war, I returned home but didn't intend to make ignitions, it just happened. I started to build a 225 hydro boat, but changed my mind after seeing Johnny Hartman's track roadster. So, I

Left to right: Bill Spalding, Tom Spalding and Wayne Horning pose for a quick photo with the Hartman/Wayne-powered GMC track roadster.

started collecting parts and pieces for a track car.

While Wayne Horning was building the GMC engine, Bill and I were making parts. We built the car in 3 weeks, and it was a masterpiece. Not only did it look good, it went like gang busters, winning every trophy dash it was in, driven by Roy Prosser. The car weighed 1375 pounds wet and boasted more than 300 horsepower.

Later, we took the track car to Bonneville and it ran 140+ mph. Both Bill and I were involved with the first open-wheeled "City of Pasadena" streamliner, built by Marvin Lee and Wayne Hoerning.

Bill got into the cam business after working for Kenny Harmon, and that's how Spalding Cams got started.

Al "Preacher" Vancich works on the front torsion bar set-up during the early construction phase of the "Hartman Torsion Bar Special."

The T frame is suspended by 11/16" diameter torsion bars, 23" long. Houdaille shocks all around. The torsion bar lash up was made by Johnny Hartman.

Below-John Hartman, himself, hard at it in his Glendale, California shop, getting the mighty roadster ready for its maiden voyage.

Here, the crew burns the midnight oil thrashing on the mighty Wayne Chevy runner. Car was built from scratch in 9 days! Johnny Hartman was never one to waste time.

Here the T body and Kurtis Kraft midget grille and nose are being aligned on the Model A Ford frame. Wheelbase was 99.5". A V8-60 radiator was used.

Below-Engine was a 6-cylinder with a 3-21/32" bore and 3-15/16" stroke. Wayne Horning built the GMC engine which was equipped with a 10:1 Wayne head, Wayne triple-carb manifold (mounting three 1-5/32" Stromberg carbs), Spalding ignition, and Winfield full-race cam. Here, Harry Warner (R), John Hartman and Wayne Horning put the finishing touches to the Hartman roadster.

Middle Right- Tom Spalding puts the touch on the Wayne "Jimmy" as the Hartman roadster is fired up prior to arriving at El Mirage. Wayne Horning's '38 Studebaker chase car is in the background.

Bottom Right-The Hartman #59 track roadster is being prepared for a pre-lakes firing by Bill and Tom Spalding on a desert road leading to El Mirage. Watching is Frank Venolia of Venolia Pistons.

The #59 Hartman track car has a new lakes number and is ready to show what it could do on the lake bed. Ran 140.18 mph "B" class speed at September 1948 SCTA meet.

The Hartman Torsion Bar Special sits up front at Carrell Speedway in Los Angeles. Car finished 4th in the first main event it ran, driven by Bob Cross.

The entire Hartman crew pictured here at Carrell Speedway, 1948. Car won 3 out of 4 trophy dashes that it appeared in. Not bad for a car that was built in 9 days!

John Hartman and Bill Spalding show off the fresh new paint job on John's GMC-powered roadster.

Bill "Sunshine" Brown drove the Hartman "B" class roadster to a speed of 140.18 mph at El Mirage in 1948. Note the two-pipe exhaust and no rear belly pan.

A later shot of old #59 displays a one-pipe collector exhaust and an aluminum rear belly pan. Belly pan helped the overall streamlining.

Tom Beatty, of Beatty & Navarro fame, puts the good eye on the SCTA's fastest roadster. This car was built and owned by Regg Schlemmer of Southgate, California. It ran a very swift 148.27 mph over the El Mirage lake course on April 25, 1948 with Neil Davis at the wheel. This car also ran up front on the California Roadster Association oval track circuit.

This beautiful (new in 1948) #555 wing tank streamliner was entered by Alex Xydias, head man and owner of So-Cal Speed Shop in Burbank, California. Power is provided by a Ford V8-60 engine for this "A" class beauty. Body consists of two P-38 drop tank halves. During the August 1948 SCTA meet, Alex's tank set an "A" class record of 130.155 mph.

This streamliner was built from two 150-gallon surplus aircraft fuel tanks which were divided in half and then fitted over the two frame units, one housing the engine and the other the driver. Power was supplied by a Merc flathead engine coupled to a '37 Ford rearend, which drove a 31-tooth sprocket, which in turn drove a 19-tooth axle sprocket mounted on a cross-shaft or rear axle.

One-inch industrial chain hooked it all together, resulting in a 2-5:1 engine to rear wheels ratio. Designed and built by Howard Johansen of Howard Cam fame, this unusual streamliner wowed the boys in 1949. The car turned 167.91 mph on a one-way run.

Bobby Meeks, one of hot rodding's top flathead V8 engine builders in the post-war era is pictured here with Bob Pierson's super-quick '36 Ford 3-window coupe. The car turned a best speed of 117.03 mph on alky at the 1948 Russetta meet. Bobbie has been associated with the Edelbrock Company for many moons!

Ernie McAfee's streamliner won the 1938 season championship. The streamliner was the first tube-frame car to run under the SCTA banner. Powered by a Winfield 4-cylinder Ford flathead, it turned in the year's fastest record speed, 137.41 mph. Two-way average speed was 132.89 mph.

Below-Another four-across elimination race at Muroc dry lake in the pre-war days. Cars were paired off in speed categories of 70-80 mph, 80-90 mph, 90-100 mph, etc. Very dusty and very exciting!

A pre-war shot of Bill Warth's 130 mph streamliner. Bill was attaining these speeds back in 1938, running a 4-cylinder Ford Winfield flathead engine. After the war, Stu Hilborn ran this car as the Hilborn Streamliner.

Ralph Schenck and his enclosed-cockpit aluminum-bodied 1938 streamliner. This was a radical approach to obtain more speed by cutting down on wind resistance back in the '30s. A Chevy 4-cylinder engine was used to run in the 130 mph class.

Bob Rufi's super slick streamliner. This car was the 1940 SCTA streamliner record holder with a two-way average of 140 mph. Bob's Chevy 4-powered beauty was also the 1940 season's class champion. Notice the aluminum wheel discs inside and out. The '25 Chevy 4-cylinder engine ran a Ford Model B crank, T pistons and a 3-port Oldsmobile head. A 143 mph one-way pass was made when establishing the 140 mph record. Bob is the one in the Navy watch cap.

The Moeller-Adams OHV heads for a Ford V8 flathead block are shown here running on the dyno. These 4-port intake and exhaust valve heads featured hemispherical combustion chambers and pumped out 200+horsepower. Heads ran a compression ratio of 10.5:1 and were manufactured by the C. K. Adams Company in Burbank, California in 1949. Spalding ignition was used on this dyno run.

No, your eyes haven't gone bad. It's just Charles Dimmitt's Cadillac V16 rear-engine "D" class roadster. It's 147-inch wheelbase chassis is fitted with two Caddy transmissions (one reversed). The engine had a total of 452 cu.in. The body is a '39 Zephyr convertible. The car made its initial lakes appearance in 1948.

This beautiful Rajo-powered T was owned by a member of a black car club from L.A. that ran Muroc back in 1935-'36. This was a super nice car.

Connie Wiedell, past president of the SCTA Gophers club, is pictured here in his Cad T roadster. Connie's T ran through the SCTA traps at 128 mph. The car turned a 133.92 mph pass with the aid of a strong wind.

A very smooth looking full-fendered street roadster from the streets of southern California back in 1942. DeSoto bumpers, sunken dash unit and big whitewalls made this little jewel a real head-turner. How about those dual horns.

A pit crew member displays the sanitary 4-port Riley set-up on this track roadster. Check the neat carb stack vents in the hood.

Flame paint jobs were popular before the war, too. This genuine tail job, sporting two head rests, was a regular at most of the pre-war lake meets.

Left-A Southern Speedway (Atlantic and Tweedy Blvd., L.A.) modified roadster track car, about 1936. From the cowl forward, these cars looked very much like the cars that ran at the old Ascot Speedway. Bodies were Model Ts with no tails. Engines were 4-cylinder, equipped with almost every special head known to man, from Rajo Ts to Chevy 3-ports.

Left Bottom-Clint Seccombe's Caddy V16-powered Model A Ford roadster gets a carburetor check at a Harpers dry lake meet in 1940. The car turned 125 mph.

Right Bottom-The Ralph Schenck streamliner as it looked in the days of pre-war lake meets. The car was one of the cleanest streamliners to run in those days.

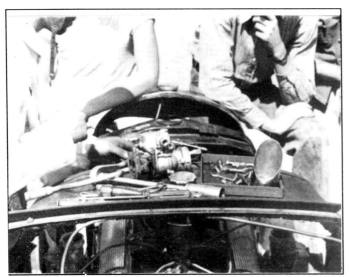

Above-An 18 year old Tom Spalding sets a carburetor float level on the Spalding Bothers streamliner during an early pre-war Muroc lakes meet.

Top Right-Tom Spalding at the wheel of the Spalding Brothers pre-war modified in 1941. Ford V8 engine is equipped with a set of Riley rocker arm heads. Mercedes blower and a pair of Stromberg carburetors handled the air/fuel mixture. This is the last car the brothers ran before the war, and it recorded a speed of 138+ mph.

Right-The Spalding Brothers '29 roadster. The car was purchased by Tom for $5 before the war. Car featured Auburn type dash and trunk-mounted gas tank. The Riley OHV equipped Ford V8 flatty ran in the 120+ class. The rear wheels and tires pictured here were borrowed from Vic Edelbrock.

T roadster equipped with a Wayne GMC 6-cylinder set-up. How would you like to get all these six carburetors in sync? The Wayne Jimmys were strong.

Left-Frank Moramoto's '29 touring car stripped and ready for action at Muroc dry lake in 1937. Frank's touring was powered by a Moeller 4-cylinder conversion.

Right-Frank Moramoto, sitting on the front wheel of his '29 touring, surrounded by all the gang. Muroc dry lake, 1937.

GMC-powered '27 T roadster with Bill Spalding behind the wheel. Binks McLean standing. This picture was taken at a 1947 lakes meet.

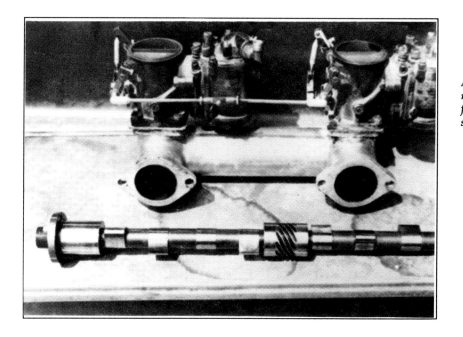

A special camshaft and Winfield dual-carb manifold used on a special McDowell head for the Ford 4-cylinder engine. Tom ran this set-up on his A in 1935.

This ad shows the ignition that started Tom Spalding in the ignition business. His 120.5 mph two-way average on Harper dry lake in 1938 was a real selling tool.

Below-Bill Spalding hangs his foot in the Jimmy-powered T roadster on a fast pass down the lake bed.

Above-The Spalding gang at a rest stop on the way home from the lakes. Phaeton belonged to the Spaldings. The rumble seat Model A coupe belonged to Pancho Stokes. Roadster owner is unknown.

The Spalding Brothers pre-war streamliner was an attraction at any lakes meet it ran. Streamliner ran the same flathead V8 that they ran in their 120 mph modified. The liner ran in the 138-140 mph class in 1939.

City of Pasadena, 1950 version, featured tubular frame, plastic skin, and sported an all new Wayne Horning GMC engine. Driven by "Puffy" Puffer, Marvin Lee's liner ran 195.652 mph at the Bonneville Nationals meet.

A 200+ mph run on Saturday ended in disaster for the car as it went out of control at the lights, did a series of endos and was destroyed. "Puffy" Puffer, hero handler, was ok thanks to the car's excellent construction.

Marvin Lee's City of Pasadena streamliner was built not only for speed but safety. The car featured Hartman torsion bar suspension front and rear, and a Halibrand quick-change rearend. A 248 cu.in. full Wayne-equipped GMC engine furnished the ponies. The engine originally ran carburetors, but a Hilborn injector was later fitted. Ran 157 mph at the 1949 Bonneville Nationals. (L to R) Bill Spalding, Wayne Horning, Marvin Lee, Tom Spalding.

Tom Beatty of blown flathead fame gives the Reg Schlemmer/ Vic Hickey #20 track roadster the once over at a 1948 CRA roadster race. This car clocked a record high speed for an American-made roadster of 148.27 mph on April 25th, 1948.

Ernie McAfee, 1938 SCTA season champ with a quick time of 137.41 mph in his 4-cylinder Winfield flathead-powered streamliner, is pictured here with his go get 'em street bike.

The Spalding Brothers super sanitary Chevy-powered track and lakes roadster of the early '50s. Tom and Bill started collecting and making parts for the car while Wayne Horning was busy building the engine. When all the parts were assembled, they built the car in 3 weeks and when finished it was a masterpiece. Frame was bent up from sheet steel to duplicate the early Essex car frame. The car weighed 1375 pounds wet. A real light weight for the time. This little beauty not only looked great, it ran like gang busters both on the track and at the lakes. Ran 146.10 mph B roadster time SCTA meet, 1949.

Tom (standing), Bill at the wheel of their just completed, soon to be painted and chromed track roadster. No, the grille does not have a tear in it, it's just the photo.

When the car was first finished, it was run with three carburetors. Notice the off-set tunnel on the hood. With the hood removed, the carburetors can be seen mounted on the left-hand side of the Chevy engine.

Rearend set-up features a Pat Warren center section, axles and hubs. Kurtis midget torsion bars were used. A Schroeder 6:1 racing steering box made the car go where it was pointed. The engine was a 1948 hi-torque Chevy with a total displacement of 248 cu.in. A 14:1 compression ratio was used. Cam and ignition were from the Spalding Brothers.

Later, six carburetors were mounted on a special manifold and were run until a Hilborn 6-port fuel injection was installed in 1950.

The mighty Spalding track roadster pictured here at an early lakes meet. (L to R) Tom Spalding, Wayne Horning, Bill Spalding. The beautiful radiator shell was built by the old master Art Ingles, who was the father of go-karts.

The 1949 Bonneville Nationals saw the Spalding Brothers B roadster on hand to try its luck on the famed salt flats. The 1949 version utilized the carbureted Wayne set-up. Car ran 144 mph one way speed. Shown here with the Spalding Brothers and Wayne Horning.

Bill Spalding is photographed with the salt flat mountains as a backdrop. This car had to be seen in person to appreciate the superb craftsmanship.

Here's the mighty Spalding track roadster with George Segar at the wheel, tearing 'em up at Carrell Speedway in 1950. This car and driver combination won every trophy dash it was in. At the state fairgrounds one mile track in Phoenix, Roy Prosser set quick time of 40.71 seconds in 1950. Roy also won the trophy dash by many lengths.

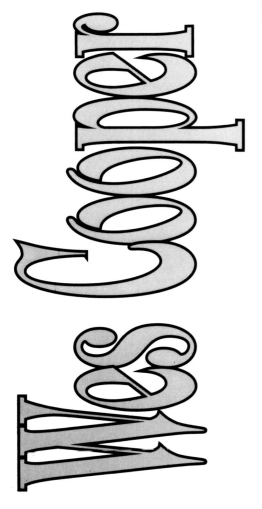

TOM: When did you first start going to the lakes?

WES: In about '35, but I didn't have anything to run until '37.

TOM: Who got you going and perked your interest?

WES: The old cam grinder from Long Beach. He learned from Clay Smith. He was a smart old guy. He ground the cam I was using later. That Cragar was just an engine I had in the'32 coupe. I took it out and I put it in the roadster, and I borrowed a guy's bedpost headers. We used to find old beds that had been thrown out. We'd cut the brass beds up and make port pipes. They'd curve down and turned out at the bottom.

That Cragar was in the '29 roadster. I borrowed the car from a kid who was working on his engine. That was in 1937. It was the first day that Ritchie Richards showed up with his '32 roadster with his flathead in it. His engine was an absolute stock 21-stud '32. He had a little bit milled off the heads and he had a single 97 on it. He had a separate coil on it with a wire running to the distributor. Everything else on it was absolutely stock. He made a run around 96 mph. It came back and ran around 97 or 98 something. I ran over to Ritchie and said, "I beat your V8." He about died. He had a fan belt comin' up, running over the pumps. Well, all he did was flip that belt off. I don't think he did anything else. He went out and turned104 mph. You wouldn't think just pushing those water pumps would do that. 104 mph was pretty good. That was the first flathead V8 to do 104 mph. That was early in 1937.

There wasn't a car in Glendale that could beat Ritchie's little V8, except one old guy who had a Cragar, old Bill Wolfe. He had an old beat up '32 roadster, and he had an old beat up Cragar in it. I was talking to his wife once. She went around with him for 7 years before they got hitched. They were out every night, and she said that nobody ever beat him in the seven years she went with him.

I got a car all ready to run the lakes and I went looking for him. I had this roadster, man it was hot. It was jerking and fuming. But I had an A box in it, I think that was what ruined me. I asked Wolfe, "You wanna go?" He said,"Hell I ain't touched it in months." He lifted the hood, and the old cover gasket was leaking. There was oil running off the engine. He fired that old muther up and winged it a couple of times. We went up to the end of the street at Brand, and all I saw were his dang taillights. I mean that muther could accelerate! I found out he had an old flathead cam in it. He had a Cragar engine in it with one carburetor, and the old heads. He said it wasn't milled. He had no compression in it. Something made it run, though, maybe the B box.

TOM: When was the first time you took a car up to the lakes?

BOB: The first time I ran, I went down to Bell Auto Parts to sign up down there. SCTA is always talking about how they started in '37. There was no SCTA when I ran that day. They gave me a number and that's all I had.

When I went up in '35, Duke Hallock had a Cragar in a '29 roadster. They broke the flange off the crank. They were the weakest one of all. They turned the crank down, and made up a complete backend, trying to press it on. They'd almost got it done, and it wouldn't go any farther, so they welded it. The flywheel was in the wrong place, but that day they ran 117 mph with it.

TOM: Did you run a sprint car out there, the roundy round type?

WES: I had one car I worked with. We won the beauty prize, but never won any races. One day we fired it up to qualify, and something busted, so we missed the main event. I forget who was out in front, but he crossed up right in the first turn, and 90% of the cars cracked up. We didn't want to lose the car. With the darn sprint car, you get the tail mashed or something, you're in trouble. That was one race we were glad we blew.

TOM: Tell about your mighty Fargo lakes roadster that ran so fast at El Mirage during the '49 lakes season. As I remember, it was on the cover of Hot Rod Magazine one issue that year.

WES: Well, my partner Hayes and I spent a great deal of time getting the little roadster ready to run that particular lakes meet. We trailered it up to El Mirage to see what it would do. It was with great expectations that we rolled it off the trailer. We fired that thing up and ran it up to the line, and it did 142 mph on the first run. The wind was coming up a little. Kong was running the start that day. He was the one that came up with those signal lights they use. There wasn't much wind, just a light breeze, but that thing was skating all over the lake. When I got down pretty close to the lights, it started going over to one side, and I was getting close to the cones. I had a 6:1 Franklin steering in it, which was too quick. I turned that thing and it still kept going over for awhile, and then it finally started going back the other way. I tell you, I thought it was about ready to spin out when it got as light as that. When I got back, here comes old Don Waite. He comes over and he yells at me, "You ran 142!" I thought he was kidding. That was a good run! That was before it was on the cover of Hot Rod Magazine, which was the September '49 issue.

TOM: How did you get into collecting heads and stuff?

WES: I got into a few rare heads, and everybody was trying to buy 'em. I have close to 25 heads now. The best one I got is that Art Sparks head. They made two heads. One was a single cam F head, and the other was a rocker arm. I've got the rocker arm. Never made any more. So that makes it rare.

TOM: When did the four cylinder stuff start picking up here ?

WES: I think when they came up with the vintage Ford four class. We were handicapped because the class we'd run in was

Car trader and lakes veteran Wes Cooper traded a Model A roadster for this cherry '32 3-window coupe. Bet he would like to have it today!

up to 250 cubes. If you made it you could run a B in the class below it, but you had to be less than 183 inches. When you start cuttin' an engines cubics, it starts droppin' off. A B runs pretty strong at 220.

TOM: The Offys were runnin' 220, but they were running some double overhead cams.

WES: Winfield said, "There are no advantages to overhead valves. An L head engine will put out just as much power as an overhead." Most of the overheads, when he was racing, didn't have over 7:1 compression. In his T, the most he ever had was 6.2:1. But when he ran the stock one on the Culver City high bank board track, he said the lower end was absolutely stock in it.

TOM: How did they pick up any oil, when it was over on the other side? They weren't running dry sump were they?

WES: There was a funnel on the back of the block, at the flywheel. You put oil into the funnel, and it ran up to the front and dropped into the pan. That's all the oil they got. He said most guys put dips on to the T rods. But his was an absolutely stock Ford lubricating system except for a bigger funnel on the back of the block. He said he did a lap on the Culver City board

track, and it was 132 mph average with that stock lower end. Then he won a hundred miler on a horse track, with that same engine. He said he had to keep it under 5000 rpm, or the center main would go out. Then he built the one with one up two down, but he said the stock one ran just about as well.

TOM: How'd the one up two down work?

WES: One and two were up at the same time, three and four were down at the same time. Then he could alter the firing. He fired it one-three-two-four. The stock one fired at one-two-four-three. Before the number one intake valve is closed the number two intake is opening. And there's nothin' left. On the A's (the ones that he built and ran), he welded the top of the water jacket in. It was over the top of the port. Then they cut the port up toward the top of the block. He had 2-1/8" intake ports in the flatheads that ran. It looked big. He said, "I put the manifold inside the engine." And that just fired one-two-four-three. Well, they went to Oakland that time, and they went out and qualified fastest. All the Offys and Millers were behind it. They went out (and it was a hundred miler), and they led it for 98 laps, and it busted a rod. They said it was turning 7000 rpm.

A very sneaky looking full belly panned '29 roadster awaits the go signal during a 1938 Muroc dry lakes meet. Wes Cooper gives the driver final instructions. Engine was a Ford 4-cylinder Cragar conversion.

No, it's not a great white shark. It's really the Beck Brothers' streamliner. This was the old Bob Rufi chassis that blew everyone's doors off back in 1940 with a 140+ mph two-way run for the record. This car was the forerunner of the post-war belly tanks.

DeFahrity in the old Jack Harvey modified. Jack was among the original SCTA members back in the early days of the sport. His little white modified with Cragar power was always one of the best appearing cars on the lake bed. The car as pictured here was running under a new owner with Ford V8 power. Pictures were shot just before WWII. Check the all-chrome rearend.

Yam Oka, Wes Cooper, and Bob Hayes look over the head gasket of their Fargo 4-port engine. This '30 Model A roadster, driven by Yam, was quick qualifier over all the hot V8 track roadsters at the Bakersfield midget track.

The Fargo 4-port head was bolted to a Ford 4-cylinder B block fitted with double Citroen connecting rods. The alky fuel was metered by four D Winfield carburetors mounted individually on the 14.5:1 comp head. A very strong runner!

This jet black B class streamliner, run at the lakes by Stu Hilborn since 1942, was originally owned by Bill Warth, early lakes runner of the '30s. Bill ran 130 mph in 1938 in this car with a Ford 4 Winfield flathead engine. Stu replaced the 4-banger with a '34 Ford V8 engine. With the new powerplant, the car ran 134 mph in 1942. Later it ran 139.96 mph with the same engine. Eddie Miller designed the 4-carburetor manifold. One Double E Stromberg and three E Strombergs were used. This set-up was used for more equal fuel distribution. Front axle is 1937 Ford with a wood and canvas fairing. Rearend gears were 3.27:1. Car ran 136 mph with Stu's experimental fuel injector. This car held the 1948 B streamliner record of 145.640 mph. Not shabby for a 21-stud flatmotor!

Here's an "under construction" shot of the Hayes-Cooper Fargo-powered roadster. Notice all the chrome goodies: shocks, spring, front axle and drag link. Would you believe $65 for all this brightwork? Those were the good old days!

The famous Bob Rufi streamliner of the 1940s was an example of ingenuity and craftsmanship. Resembling the post-war belly tank, this little beauty was indeed a lakes masterpiece for the time. Powered by 1925 Chevrolet 4-cylinder engine, it ran a Ford Model B crankshaft, Model T Ford rods, and a 3-port Oldsmobile head. Also ran a special Tornado head. The driver was completely enclosed behind a plexiglass canopy. A very tight fit, indeed, as can be seen in the photo. The front wheels were fitted with aluminum discs inside and out for less drag. The rear wheels were enclosed with beautiful streamlined wheel parts for some meets. All in all, a very compact and efficient set-up. It's little wonder it set the lakes boys on their ears when Bob's little projectile ran over 143 mph in 1940 and ended up with the 1940 SCTA streamliner record for two-way average of 140 mph.

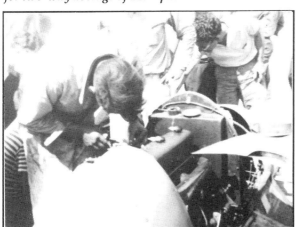

In 1938, Ralph Schenck put together this all aluminum, fully enclosed lakes streamliner. Built to run a Chevrolet 4-cylinder engine, this construction masterpiece was acknowledged to be one of the cleanest and most superbly built cars running on the dry lakes prior to WWII. Following WWII, Ralph's little jewel surfaced again, running several Russetta meets with a V8 engine and new owner. The car was featured on the July 1950 Hot Rod Magazine cover.

This pre-war Glendale Sidewinder club '29 roadster is getting a coupon from a Glendale motorcycle officer on Brand Blvd., (probably for having no windshield). From the looks of the cars in the background, the year is about 1938 or '39. Notice the Red Car tracks running down the center of Glendale's main drag, Brand Blvd.

Wes Cooper's super clean '32 Ford roadster that he drove on the street. Engine was 4-cylinder Ford with a Cragar OHV head. Carburetion was handled by a single SD Winfield carburetor. Check that 1942 California license plate. Only 4 numbers and 1 letter. Ha! No grid-lock back then!

Right and left-hand side of Riley 2-port head set-up, running two Winfield Model S carburetors. This engine was running in a Model A sedan after WWII.

One of Wes Cooper's many cars. He had owned more than 50 by 1947. This little 3-window '32 was his for $185 in 1937. Later, he put a '32 roadster body on the chassis. The engine has a Miller head. Port cover plates were made by Murphy.

This "old time" Cragar-powered race car, owned by Wes Cooper before the war, was towed to the lakes by his brand new '41 Ford club coupe. Wes is shown at speed in old #266. From the looks of the photos, the lake bed was far from crowded.

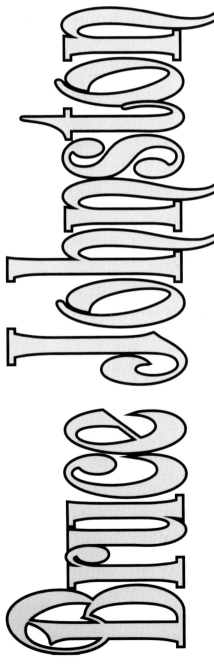

Bruce Johnston

BRUCE: The first time I went to the lakes was 1937. I was still in high school then. I remember going with my rich buddy Betry who had the forerunner of the speed shop over on Colorado, by Bob's Big Boy restaurant in Glendale. It was long before the war, 'cause when Winfield closed the carburetor factory, Betry bought all the parts. Betry used to make adaptations on the stock V8 manifolds. Had tubes all over the outside. I don't know what they did. They were kind of a joke to all of us, but he seemed to sell them. They did something with these little tubes with screens in them. Sold heads for the Fords, the air cooled ones. Bronze or brass. I had a set that nobody has seen since. They were for the early 21-stud. They were water cooled. They had an aluminum jacket bolted onto the bronze head. That was the only set I have ever seen. Kong used to borrow them, because he never owned a set of heads. They were the only ones that were high enough compression for him.

My first time at the lakes, I remember it was pretty wild. Guys running every direction. They had a few fatalities. I don't think we even had an ambulance then. That was on Muroc. We never ran at El Mirage at all. It was Muroc, Harper and Rosemond that we used. Muroc was the best.

We ran there in '41. I went up there once just before I went in the army in '42. Bud Rose and I took the race car up there. And the army was there. Nobody stopped us. We just went out and ran it. I remember an airplane going over so low, we could see the guy and his mustache in the cockpit looking us over. Nobody told us to get off, and I guess that we were one of the last to run on the lake.

That was before they stopped racing. I'd already gotten interested in oval track by then, although I was still running at the lakes. I had a roadster, and my oval tracker, which was a streamliner then. There were only three classifications... roadster, modified and a streamliner. A modified was a roadster, basically, that had been narrowed. The tail is what made it a streamliner. There were four or five of us that ran. Mel Leighton ran his, I ran mine, and there was another guy with a Crager called "Sumpin Special." Mel lived in Santa Barbara and was secretary at SCTA, I think. We used to have our meetings down at Clifton's Cafeteria, with the waterfall. I belonged to the Sidewinders then. I was the club rep, so I had to go to all the SCTA meetings. In fact, our little club here, the Super 4s, we got probably the most pre-war racers of any club. Dave Martin, myself, Cooper, Kong. There's four of us in that one club that ran before the war. And I believe there is only one other guy in SCTA that ran. That was Hank Nagley.

TOM: Did you run mostly four cylinder stuff?

BRUCE: My roadster was a V8. Well, that was my third roadster. My first was a Crager; I built a real exotic thing with a stroked crank and everything. I gutted it, welded the body to the frame. I thought making it light was the way to go...which it wasn't. I flipped a rod right out the side of it. Cut it in two practicing, before I ever timed it.

TOM: You must have run when they were running those 4- abreast eliminations.

BRUCE: We did. And then also sometimes it was 2-abreast. I remember the day Vic Edelbrock set the roadster record of 121 mph. I think it was a guy in our club, Roger Blanche who had a flathead four. He and Vic had run 119 mph, and for some reason they weren't going to let him run against Edelbrock. So, he lined up beside Edelbrock and whoever else it was, and went off, and Roger beat them both. They said his dust made them shut off and they banned him at the next lakes. But, it kind of upset everybody...that B flathead, beating Edelbrock's V8.

Bill Warth and McAfee had a flathead that ran up in the 130 mph class back in the 1930s. Of course, Rufi ran a 140+ mph. I think it was at Harper. Harper was hard as cement. I understand they scraped it all off now. The others were mud, but Harper was something different. White, like concrete, and you could leave black rubber marks, it was so hard.

TOM: You know, I have only seen one or two pictures of Rufi's streamliner with those trick skirts on the rear wheels.

BRUCE: I've got one or two pictures. It's sitting there with the skirts on it the day he set the record. A lot of people don't realize it, but I don't think he ran the Olds head. There's a guy named Lee Chappel, and he had a Tornado head. Some young guy made it at Trade Tech. LA high school made the patterns. It looked like an Olds, but had bigger valves and bigger ports. I believe that's what, Rufi had. Lee later moved up to the bay area and had a speed shop. He made an overhead streamliner there, after the war.

Phil Remington's consistently quick B streamliner at a Muroc dry lakes meet prior to WWII. Phil was a member of the Low Flyers club.

TOM: Another thing I noticed about the Rufi car was that he had solid wheel discs on both sides.

BRUCE: He was thinking when he made that, and I think they made him take the full canopy off in case he got upsidedown or had a fire. The thing was quite small. Very short with a narrow tread.

TOM: But it was beautiful when he was inside with the canopy down. It was slippery. Must have handled fairly well. He did 140 in it.

BRUCE: I remember he used to change the head gasket on every run. There are only ten bolts on a Chevy. Some of those old Chevys ran real well.

TOM: Wally Parks was saying how he was driving somebody's car one day in one of those eliminations, and he got down there and was doing real great. He hit that first wire, and then backed off...and then everyone went by him...and he suddenly realized he had to trip another wire.

BRUCE: There used to be a quarter mile trap. Now, it's 132 feet, which is 1/10 mile. But, you had to go the full quarter then, and you ran over the wire. Later on, when we used to race back east with the sprinters, it was a hose you ran over...like the dinger at the gas stations. And that punched the clock. We had the idea that if you hit the hose near the fence, starting the clock and close to the clock finishing, you gained 1 or 2 hundreths because of the length of the air hose. I don't know if it made any difference.

TOM: When did you go to Bonneville the first time?

BRUCE: After I quit oval track running, and I raced boats for awhile. I set the fastest lap ever turned at the Salton Sea. Of course, it's been beaten now, probably by an outboard. One year I ran down there with a factory Ford 427, that they guaranteed would go about three days at 6000. It went about three hours, and fell apart, broke the crank. So I switched back to a hemi. Boat racing is funny. You can't run hard all the way, like you do in a car. They are climbing a hill all the way, pulling like hell, and they just won't live.

Along in there I started running this vintage oval track. I kind of founded the Western Racing Association. I later dropped out of it and started looking for something to do and I thought, maybe the lakes would be the place to go. You can run at any dollar level, and there is no hassle.

Nobody is hurrying you up. Sit in line all day, if you want. Nobody cares if you run or if you don't run. I thought I'd take my oval tracker up there. So I talked to a couple of people about it, and they said, "Just put a roll bar on it and bring it up."

I installed a roll bar and took it to the lakes. Of course, I also installed a parachute and a fire extinguisher. The first run I made, it didn't run for beans. It ran about 145 at 4500 rpm. I thought, the next run I'll cut 'em a good one, so I ran through again, and it went from 4500 up to 6200 rpm. And it only picked up two miles an hour. That's when I learned about wheel spin. From there on, the only way to go faster was to raise the gear and pour the nitro to it, and just spin the tires harder.

Of course, now you're not allowed to run nitro in that class. I was kind of instrumental in banning it, 'cause all it does is...if I run 30%, then you'll run 40%...then I'll put in 50%, and we'll both have broken engines.

TOM: You ran up until the war?

BRUCE: Yes, and then I got bit pretty bad by the oval trackers. Just before the war, I started racing down at South Gate with my Riley 4-port race car. I started going to a few midget races, and I got interested in them.

At the end of the war, I was stationed at Muroc. The bomb had been dropped, and I could see the war was going to be over, and I started building a race car on the air base in the shop there. I made the frame rails and got a body from Frank Kurtis before he built his tube frame midgets. I built it with a V8 60, and when I got

out in February of '46, I was almost ready to run.

Well, I got a terrible shock. I'd been racing on pavement at South Gate with my Riley, and the midgets run dirt. I had visions of blowing everybody off. Boy, I did everything, but get in the grandstands. I had no idea where I was going. They had what we thought were giant purses compared to pre-war. So I promptly decided I'd better hire a driver and get some of this big money. That year we ran the midget 60, and in mid '47 I got an Offy. I got that running sometime late in '47. Mac Hellings was driving.

We went east. We picked up Langhorn, the hundred miler and a bunch more of them back there at the end of the season.

TOM: Did you run the 16th Street Speedway across from the Indy 500 track?

BRUCE: Oh yeah. I ran around there in '48, (URA). In fact, if I remember right, Mac won the championship. URA and I didn't get along too well. So, I went back to AAA. In '49 we spent the whole year back east. We used to stay around Chicago at Crown Point, and we could run every night of the week.

I usually ran Kokomo on Sunday, and quite often I'd take Monday off to work on it. Then Tuesday we'd hit St. Louis. Wednesday was Soldiers Field, Chicago. Thursday we had a choice of about four or five places: Lafayette, Terra Haute, and some others. Johnny Parsons and I were living in the same house for awhile, and he sat down and figured we averaged 20 miles an hour — counting eating, sleeping and everything. We never had the trailer off the car. We were always moving. Occasionally, we'd break the deal and go off and run in Ohio, Detroit, or if we got real bored we could go east and run the ARDC around Hindgecliff Stadium. We went to the half mile at Thompson Connecticut, Oswego, New York, and a lot in between. The midgets finally died out, and I went back to to big cars, my first love.

I built a blown Offy midget engine for a sprinter. There were a few of them around. Mine was one of the first, and it worked very well. But there wasn't enough racing, so I told AAA zone rep Gordon Betz I had to run elsewhere.

He said, "I don't blame you."

The first time we ran it, we went down to Carrell Speedway, and ran a match race against a roadster. At that time, I think it was Howard Johansen's roadster that was quick. We were warming it up. I was driving, taking hot laps, and was running under his track record. These guys couldn't believe it, with that little engine. I came in and Dempsy Wilson was going to drive. The guys were laughing because I had knobby tires. By this time, the track got slick and at the last minute I stuck on some big grooved slicks. They'd been doing quite a bit of lipping off about their roadsters.

Dempsey says, "What'll I do?"

We were originally going to let the roadster win.

110

Then the next week, we'd come back and the sprint car would win. I said, "Lap him, if you can."

He damn near lapped him in three laps. Boy, you could hear a pin drop. Then I ran a few races with Dempsey driving it.

TOM: When did you have your first A-V8?

BRUCE: The first one I gave a hundred dollars for, and got ripped off pretty bad. It was a junk engine. He was telling me how keen it was. That was '39 maybe.

I sold that to Billy Huth, who has Willow Springs now. He financed it at the bank. Payments were $7.00 a month, and he couldn't make them. I sold it to him when he was 15 or 16, and still in high school.

I built another one. I traded that for a '32 without a body. I kept my engine, to put in the '32. I couldn't find a roadster body right off, so I put a '28 pickup body on it. I cut the bottom out of the bed, so I could set it a little lower.

Shortly after that, I got a '28 or '29 roadster body, and put it on and kept it up until the war. It was my only transportation. I was working in a machine shop at night in Pasadena. That was in '41. I got 50 cents an hour. I quit and went to work for Lockheed because I could work days and got a penny an hour more.

Then I got a passenger car, a '36 Ford coupe. I ran it in a stock car race in South Gate. At the last minute, I couldn't go. I let Kong and a friend of mine, Paul Pold drive. The rules said you could run any manifold, so we put an Edelbrock on it. It was a full race engine for the day. They made him take it off at the last minute, so they got a stock manifold out of the parking lot. I guess they stole it.

At the start of the race, Paul came from last to first in the second lap; finally fried the engine and blew the head gaskets. They couldn't run the fan after they changed manifolds 'cause it hit the radiator. They were towing it home with the head gaskets blown, and someone ran into it. It went though the race without a dent, and someone ran into it on the way home! That was my only car for a long time.

Finally, in about '53 I got disgusted with oval track racing. Purses were down. The last year I ran the sprinter was in IMCA, which was considered outlaw then. I owned it, drove it, worked on it, towed it...everything. I wasn't making any money at the end of the year. All I had was a worn out race car, and no money to rebuild it.

I sold a supercharged Offenhauser and a modern sprinter for $1500. The same car today would be worth who knows how much.

A while back at the lakes, Frank Moromoto came up with a guy, who said he had the first Rileys, and Stellings said, no, he did. Anyway, there weren't too many of 'em made. There were a few around town. I doubt if he made a half dozen sets. And Riley also made a complete V8 engine, a few of which exist yet today. He used a Ford crank and rods. He made the case and the block. It was a single overhead cam on each bank. Some Ford dealers in Portugal sponsored it to run in road races. He made a later version. Riley made a lot of stuff. He made an outboard he worked on. It finally bankrupted him. He was trying to sell it to the military, and he got involved with a bunch of shysters that were going to promote it. They left him with all the bills, and they took the money...the usual story. It was a 5-cylinder outboard. The radials set horizontal. Water cooled. I remember he was working on it all during the war. Then he started making his Riley carburetors, and everybody bought them for the Offys.

There were no Winfields available and they ran faster than the Winfields. Then, Hilborn injectors kind of put carburetors out of business.

We were at Harper on a Saturday. It was '40 or '41. We used to lay on the ground in sleeping bags. Pretty primitive then. Of course we were young. This guy in our club, his name is Chuck Green, had a nice '32 roadster. He towed it with a '36 convertible. He got there and it was dark. He fired up this roadster, and we could hear him running around the lakes...no lights. Just screaming in low gear. It was making a circle and he didn't realize it, and he came around and ran right into the back of his own tow car. Demolished the '32, and he went flying out. This was all a few feet from us where we were sleeping. It destroyed both cars and broke both his legs.

I remember at one of the early SCTA lake meets where no coupes or sedans were allowed. Nothing with fenders. And this '37 shows up, with the fenders off. It was a convertible. No top, and the windshield had been chopped, as I remember. Everyone was laughing, because 6-cylinder Chevys are 70 mile an hour cars. The thing went 109 mph. It really stopped everybody. I think that was the forerunner of the Wayne Horning head. Horning took one to Oakland before the war for a stock car race, and it went like a rocket. It wasn't stock either. Of course, everyone was cheating. They were all running for second, so they wouldn't get torn down.

TOM: I remember when the CRA was running and Johansen was running. Those guys had the engine stuffed back so far that you couldn't check the back cylinders. You couldn't get into them. The ones you could get at were stock bore.

BRUCE: The other ones were oversize?

TOM: Yeah. And Johansen ran everything oddball. He was the greatest guy in the world. You'd love Howard, 'cause he was a practical guy. I remember I was down there one day and he said, "Come on, I've got to go over to this surplus store." They had a lot of stuff, at the time. He'd walk through this place, and he had it all visualized what he was going to put together. At SAC headquarters in Omaha was Fort Crook. Right next door was the big airplane factory. After the war, they were going to close it all down. They had grinders, but they weren't cam grinders. Howard bought several and converted them to automatic cam grinders.

I went down there one day. Remember when they first started coming out with accessory wheels? He was making steel wheels. They'd flame cut the slots in them. He wanted the things dished. Some guy was charging 50 cents a pop to dish them. He said, "Heck with that," so he went over and got a couple of surplus aircraft hydraulic cylinders and made his own.

And then, when he'd weld the center sections in and he had a thing set up with a mix master rheostat to control the welder. He also made his own chrome plating plant.

BRUCE: You know there were a lot of people like him throughout the country in the depression days. Ak Sowers is a good example. He built that midget engine. Al was a little primitive, but it got the job done.

Well, like Dryer in Indianapolis. He built the engines. He built a two-cam engine and even hammered out his own cars, and did that all his life. That's all he ever did.

Another one was Hosterman, that built the HAL engine. And there was a guy named Green. Pop Green. I never knew his name. He made heads and all kinds of stuff. And of course, Fronty, the Chevrolet brothers with their T items. They built some exotic Indy engines before they went into the T.

TOM: That always amused me. The Chevrolet brothers building Ford stuff.

BRUCE: But there were guys like that throughout the country. And there's many one-of-a-kind engines. I used to run into back east. Some of them two cams, some of them single cams. There was a guy in Chicago who had a single cam engine. Crudest old race car, but it won a lot of races.

Another example was John Gerber in Iowa. He built two race cars. They were really primitive at first. Little bobtails, and you sat down beside the drive shaft. He was using Chevy 4s, but they were super light, and they handled well. And he'd beat everybody. But the Chevys would blow up, so then he started building his own engine. It still looked like a Chevy 4, only it had five mains and his own head with extra head bolts. I got to know him in later years, and those things were darn near unbeatable. Especially in long races. They were very dependable.

He and Maynard Clark used to tour the country with these things. They had a Willys 2-door. This was when Willys were bigger cars, and the one seat flopped down where one of them could sleep while the one drove. They'd always show up with their bib overalls and straw hats, and a little pet pig, and blow everybody off. They showed up at Winchester, a AAA race, and they wouldn't let them run these bobtails. They were so primitive. Gerber finally said, "I'll tell you what. If we don't qualify 1-2, we'll load up and go home. They all laughed, and they sat 1-2 and they ran 1-2. Blew everybody off. Then they went to the east coast, and beat everybody.

John Gerber was telling me once that a guy had made them some new rod bolts out of some German steel. They got the car all done, and they were going racing the next day. They were sitting around having a beer, and they heard this "plink." They looked all over and couldn't figure out what it was. Pretty soon they heard it again. Somebody said it came out of the engine. They pulled it down, and the rod bolts were snapping. They were too hard and sitting there under a load. They broke. They put the old bolts in and went racing. Never a dull moment in the racing game!

Vic Edelbrock Sr. in his '32 Ford roadster (#13) shown here at Muroc dry lake. Vic was a regular at all the 1940s pre-war lake meets where he fine-tuned his line of flathead V8 speed equipment. The Edelbrock name is known world-wide in automotive circles, with Vic Jr. heading up the very successful Edelbrock Company today.

A pre-war '30 Model A roadster, running a Murphy rocker arm head and SR Winfield carburetor. These heads were very rare! This roadster was driven to the lake bed, fenders and headlights removed, windshield laid back and presto, time to go racing!

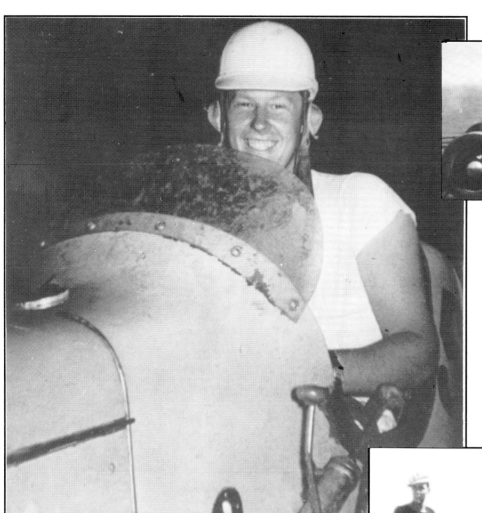

Above-How about 130+ mph one way with a 4-cylinder Ford Winfield flathead engine back in 1938! Here's a car that did it: Bill Warth's super looking streamliner. Car was purchased later by Stu Hilborn and was seen at many lake meets after the war.

Left-Bruce Johnston in a Roy Richter-built midget, running a Jr. Cragar engine (a rocker arm Continental) San Diego, California, 1941-'42 season.

Not every trip down the course turned out successful. Here's a '32 roadster that looks a little worse for wear. Muroc, 1939.

Tom Spalding at the wheel of the Spalding Brothers pre-war streamliner. Ran 126 mph. Tom stated, "It's a good thing we didn't go any faster or we would have flown for sure!"

Right- Bruce Johnston's and Melvin Short's Cragar at Muroc dry lake in 1939. A rod ventilated the block just before this photo was taken.

The Danny Sakai V8-powered modified, 1940. Engine ran Mal Ord heads and manifold. The car was later owned by Willit Brown.

Ben Martin, Glendale Sidewinders club member, waits his turn to run at a 1939 Muroc lakes meet. His '29 roadster ran a Riley 2-port and turned a speed of 109 mph.

Another typical modified T bobtail. Many cars similar to this ran the lakes in those early days before WWII. Check the fuel pressure pump and the timing slip taped to the cowl.

In the '40s, the top four cars in a given speed category were raced together to determine the fastest car. Here (left to right) are Vic Edelbrock, Bill Spalding, Binks McLean and Clint Seccombe getting it on down Harpers dry lake bed. Seccombe, in his Caddy V16-powered roadster, was the winner with a speed of 125 mph.

A 2-port Riley powered this bobtail T, owned by Ben Martin of the Glendale Sidewinders club. Nothing fancy, just go as fast as you can and have fun. Muroc, late '30s.

Above- Bruce Johnston, the tall one, and a group of the pre-war Glendale Sidewinders surrounding Bill Martin's 4-port Riley. The grille was made from his mother's refrigerator shelf.

Bill Martin's 4-port Riley had fast time for the day of 125 mph. Muroc dry lake bed, 1940.

Those were the days; get some rays, run your car and have fun! That's what these Glendale Sidewinder members are doing at this pre-war Muroc meet.

Four-cylinder Cragar running dual Winfield carburetors. This is a typical set-up run at Southern Ascot Speedway, Atlantic & Tweedy Blvds., prior to WWII.

Below Right- "Skip-It", an unusual custom 2-man car seen at many of the pre-war lake meets. The trick grille is either a '37 or '38 Oldsmobile. Check those flames.

Below- Need to change gears? Easy, just jack up the closest stocker and swap the wheels to your roadster. Bruce Johnston is shown doing the change on his roadster.

A very rare '31 Ford tudor phaeton running a Riley 2-port conversion. This little gem drove to the meet, pulled off the fenders and went racing. Didn't even bother to remove the headlights.

This super sand modified of Danny Sakai was a top runner during the 1940-'41 meets, running in the 128-130 mph bracket.

Below Left- You didn't always drive to the lakes even back in 1940-'41. Some of the guys flew in private. This Command-Air, powered by a OX5 engine, showed up at Rosemond and all the troops wanted a ride to see the course from the air. For those that did, it was a ball.

Below- Mel Short, Glendale Sidewinders, changes plugs on Bruce Johnston's '29 roadster at Muroc in 1940.

Most of the pre-war cars were built on a budget. Speed equipment was available for engines, but body and chassis stuff had to be fabricated by hand. This '29 roadster had a belly pan fabricated from fabric stretched over a framework and drawn tight with aircraft dope. Wonder what happened if there was a fire?

Bruce Johnston, Glendale Sidewinders, holds the door shut on his '29 roadster after turning a speed of 110.02 mph at Muroc, 1941.

Mel Short (foreground) and Bruce Johnston get ready for a pass. Engine was a '36 Ford 21-stud V8 with Fedral-Mogul water cooled heads, Edelbrock manifold and Winfield cam. It turned 110.02 mph at Muroc in 1941.

Making a very rare lakes appearance was this Ford V8 front-drive Indianapolis car.

This is a pre-war photo of the modified that is now owned by Art Chrisman and can be seen in its restored beauty running at many nostalgia drag races around the country today.

Typical starting line scene just following
WWII at El Mirage, as this '32 roadster is
getting set for a run through the lights.
Roadsters everywhere you look!

A pre-war scene at Muroc dry lake as this 4-cylinder Ford
modified gets ready for a run. Check out the PA system — horns
on the A sedan. Wild, huh?

With Bill Daily driving, the Xydias/Batchelor 275 cu.in. C class
streamliner ran 210 mph one way on the way to a new Bonneville
Nationals 2-way record of 208.9271 mph. The Edelbrock-equipped
engine ran a Kong ignition and Winfield cam.

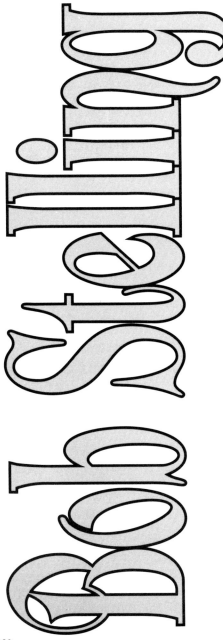

Bob Stelling

TOM: When did you first start going to the lakes?

BOB: In 1935 when I was in high school. Through '39 I was pretty steady into it, running Muroc, and Rosemond some of the time.

TOM: When did you meet Tom Spalding?

BOB: It was sometime around '36 or '37. Tom and Bill were going to Curtis Wright aircraft school. I built my first A-V8 about that time. I bought a new '32 crossmember from Ford. You could get 'em cheap. I think I paid $3.25 for mine. A '32 frame was much wider than a Model A, so I cut it off about an inch and a half from either side and V 'ed it out. Of course it was taller too, so I notched it. It made a great installation. Then I used a '32 mount on the rear of that cross member. I drove that car for about a year, then I sold it to a guy named Beeman. I got big bucks for it, maybe $375. That was a lot of dough in those days. Never saw him or the car after that.

TOM: Where'd you guys go street racing?

BOB: Right here in the San Fernando Valley. We'd go out Sunday morning and take the race cars. We'd go with straight pipes on the Offys and the whole works. We would measure off a stretch out there by the Church. There was a high school named Mother Cabrini, about Glenoaks Blvd. and Buena Vista. It's Woodbury College now. You could go by Hansen Dam clear out to Van Nuys Blvd. I think the best we got going was about 125 mph in a stretch. Try doing that now!

One Sunday, on Glenoaks, I had the race car out there (the midget...Hendricks had his midget and Prickett had his midget). For some reason or other I was up on the trailer getting ready to unload my car when here comes the highway patrol, and old Perry Grimm comes a sailin' by at about120 mph past this highway patrol officer, and he kept his foot in it all the way home to Prickett's place and got away. Hendricks was a cop at the time, and I guess they about put him in jail for aiding and abetting. The highway patrol didn't approve of that!

TOM: Did the police give you much hassel when you were street racing the roadsters?

BOB: Never did. I never got caught. We used to race on Lincoln Blvd too. That was a pretty wild setup. The guys would mainly hang out at the Barrel drive-in over there on Beverly Blvd. It was about 3 or 4 blocks off of La Brea.

The Jantzen Beach midget track in Portland, Oregon was a good race area. We raced there quite a bit. There was a guy up there by the name of Ryan that promoted it. He was a good honest promoter.

TOM: I told you about the time that I saw the first Offy at Jantzen Beach, didn't I? The press made a big deal that the Offy was going to be coming. At that time, they were running all the 4-cylinder Stars and the Elto 460's and anything else that would fit the rules. They would run on Thursday night, and I would always be absent from school on Friday, because I'd hitch hike all the way from Salem to Portland all by myself, go to the races and hitch hike all the way back by myself. Then I'd be thrashed the next day.

This particular night, everybody had qualified...and still no Offy. And all of a sudden in the pits we hear vroomm, varoomm...and there's this Offy sittin' there. No paint on it, just bare aluminum. Man, it looked fast. They went out and while they were running warm-up laps, they broke the track record. I remember that so well.

It wasn't until about 20 years later that I found out why those guys were so darn late. I was talkin' to Allen Heath, and he said those guys were bringing it down from the Seattle/Tacoma area. They were towing the midget on the Washington side of the Columbia River and they had never fired the car. So they whipped it off the trailer and fired it up. They're going flat-out and, wouldn't you know it, they got stopped by the local police. They ran 'em in and fined 'em, and were going to throw them in jail, until they explained that they had to be at Jantzen Beach to race, so the judge let them go. And that's why they were so late.

BOB: We did that one time going to Bakersfield. We had just overhauled a car and we were kind of late. Johnny Parsons was driving the car for me. We got off the top of the Ridge Route and unloaded the darn thing and he drove it all the way down to the track in Bakersfield. We'd get going about 70-80 mph in the wagon and he'd come flyin' by us, and we'd try and get him to slow down. But no dice. He drove it all the way to the Bakersfield track, about 15 miles. That was a pretty common practice back then.

TOM: How'd you get into the business with Mac Hellings?

BOB: Well, when Hellings got killed, I was running Barker's business, along with ours over in Glendale. And Barker was killed with Mac and some other fellow that was supposed to be flying the airplane. They were going to Bay Meadows for a race. They just flew it into the mountain up there in Gorman. They got into a canyon and couldn't turn it around. Mac had a couple hundred hours and I'm surprised he let himself get into that. He probably wasn't paying attention. Ed Elliott came into the shop the next day and said, "Have you heard anything from the guys? We were flying over Gorman and we saw them down below us. Nobody has seen them since then." They got the search going and it took them 2 or 3 days to find them. After a year or two, the business was going bad, the guy who was running it wasn't doing the job. So I took that over too. Fortunately we made a little money on other things to put in it and saved it for awhile.

Jack Harvey's Cragar-powered modified at a Muroc meet in the early days of SCTA competition. A very neat and well constructed car.

We were making all the rocker arms for B & B (Barker). We made gear boxes too. I thought about that all the time on the ship...the gearboxes. I sold about 400 of 'em, which was a pretty good production.

TOM: How did you happen to get into the midget stuff?

BOB: I never had anybody who was really successful to give me any advice, and I really didn't know anybody until after I got the midget. For some reason or another old Russ Garnet and I kind of hit it off. Russ wouldn't tell me what to do, but he'd say, "If this was mine, I would do this." It worked so well that I began to respect somebody with a little bit of experience. He helped me an awful lot.

You mentioned Tom and Bill Spalding, well I've gotta tell you, everything Tom and Bill put together was so beautiful, so meticulous. I wondered which one of them was the guiding light. They made a good combination. Probably what one didn't think of the

other one did. The roadster and streamliner they built were works of art. They built a log type manifold for the flathead, and that was a beautiful piece of work. It ran too, it was a good manifold. Some of those ignitions Tom built, the workmanship was out of this world!

TOM: You worked for Lockheed, then?

BOB: Yes, before the war, and almost 'til the end of the war.

TOM: You must have driven some of your roadsters to work?

BOB: The '32 yeah. I sold the '32 roadster to Harry Kamamura They shipped him out, and I never did know what happened to him. It's funny...some of those Japanese guys went to the concentration camps and nobody ever kept in touch with them after the war. I asked about some of the guys, but nobody really kept in touch after that. It's a shame.

This car appears to be the Jack Harvey modified but running a different engine set-up. Possibly a V8 Ford. Check the GIs looking over the car. With those hats, it's gotta be just before WWII.

Bob Stelling's '35 Ford convertible towed Lee Findley's Winfield flathead '29 roadster to Muroc all the way from Glendale to run at this 1935 lakes meet. How about the two rumble seat passengers, one with a helmet and goggles and the other a typical dress style hat. Oh my!

Bob Stelling in his stripped-down '35 Ford convert, complete with wide white walls, ready to make a pass down Muroc dry lake bed. Bob's passenger was Bill Butterfield, who today is a retired Air Force general. The '35 turned a Muroc Timing Association speed of 84.30 mph on June 22, 1935.

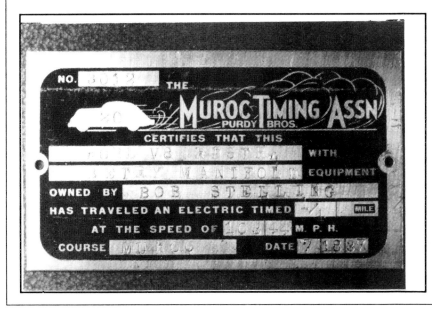

In 1937, Bob Stelling of Stelling & Hellings Air Cleaner fame, owned this fine looking '32 Ford roadster in both street and racing attire. Bob turned 103.44 mph in his '32 at Muroc dry lake, timed by the Purdy Brothers on July 12th, 1937. Stock engine with Betry manifold.

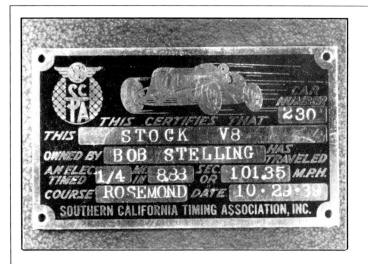
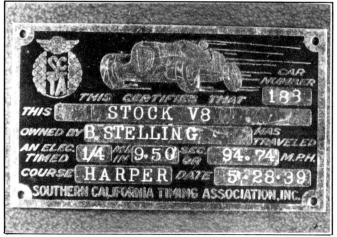

Bob Stelling timing tags from Muroc
Timing Association and early SCTA.
Those early lakes events were run on
Muroc, Harpers and Rosemond dry lakes
in the southern California desert area.

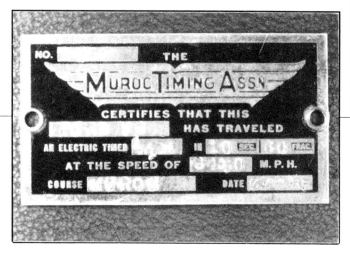

Left-On your mark, get set .... A line of
roadsters ready to have at it side by side
in an early lakes elimination race.
Qualification runs determined in what
class you would run.

Right- A sharp looking early
lakes modified waits in line
at Muroc during a pre-war
lakes meet. Car looks very
much like the modified later
run by Karl Orr.

126

TELLING IT LIKE IT IS

T-Shirts are as much a tradition in hot rodding as flathead V8's and dropped axles. In recent years, it has become popular to make a statement with the T, and that's exactly what our special line of T-shirts and Jerseys do. Since we introduced this line recently, the demand has been overwhelming, now you can get your personal copy through the mails. Top quality, American made, sizes hold very true. These are white T's, suitable for just hanging around or ocassional formal wear. The Traditional versions are available with or without our HOT ROD MECHANIX or CUSTOM CAR magazine words on the back, be sure and tell us with or without logo!

TRADITIONAL
"Real Street Rods Are Driven!"
"Real Custom Cars Are Driven!"

HOT COLORS
"Hot Rods And Rock & Roll"
"Custom Cars And Rock & Roll" (neon)

You can get these as T-Shirts, Jerseys, or Tank Tops. Sizes S,M,L,XL,XXL

TANKS	$10 plus $1 Shipping
T's	$12 plus $1 Shipping
JERSEYS	$15 plus $1 Shipping

(1 Through 4: Not available in Jersey)

"Real Street Rods Are Driven"
is available in Tanks, T-shirts, & Jerseys.

Hot Rod Mechanix Featured on the back!

Mastercard/Visa orders 1-800-782-0539

Name_____Phone_____

Street_____

City_____State____Zip_____

Mastercard/Visa #_____Exp._____

Signed_____

(Allow 4-6 weeks delivery. Canadian add $3 shipping, Foreign add $5)

Please send me:

T-SHIRT(s)____Size(s)____Design____with/WO Logo____

JERSEY(s)____Size(s)____Design____with/WO Logo____

TANKTOP(s)____Size(s)____Design____with/WO Logo____

127

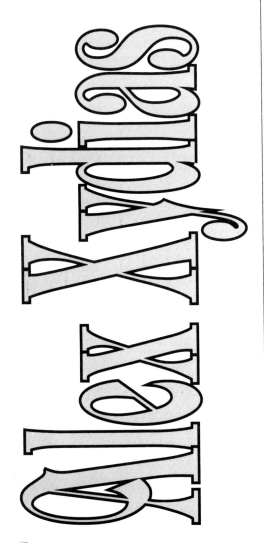

Our tank received more awards than any car ever at Bonneville. We got three 1st places, 2 records, and the Best Appearing Car and Crew. We won six awards in one meet in 1953, I believe. This was when Clyde Sturney and I ran it together. We were running a flathead, and as it turned out this was the final year of the Ford flathead V8. We ran it against Ray Brown's hemi Chrysler belly tank. He had the record, but we had the fastest one-way time. It ran 199 something.

TOM: How big an engine, do you remember?

ALEX: It wasn't one of those huge huge engines. It might have been 3/8. What was that 296 or something? It was less than 300, that's for sure. I know that the B engines were up to 254 inches. And the A engines were over that.
The remarkable thing was that we took three engines. We ran the V8 60 first. The same V8 60 that I always had. We ran it and set the record, and got first in class. Then we ran Clyde's B engine that we built in the speed shop. He got the record in B class, and also top speed in B class. Then we ran the C engine, the big V8, and got first place in it but we couldn't get the record. I think Bobby had slipped a little nitro in it. We had never run nitro before, but I think Bobby might have, to try to beat Ray Brown. Brown was running the darn Chrysler, and we were actually competing against a Chrysler with a flathead. It was amazing!
So we got six awards. We also got the tool boxes for Best Appearing Car and Crew.

TOM: You were actually running alcohol?

ALEX: We did that and everything else. That final run was on a Sunday morning, the last day. We had already run in the other two classes. First of all we ran the V8 60 the first day and broke the existing record, so we could run Tuesday morning for record run. As soon as the record run was over, we ran back to the motel and changed engines again, and got the B engine out in time to run and qualify for record run the next morning. Geeze, we were changing three engines. Everyone one of 'em won its class, and two of 'em got the record.

TOM: Where were you changing engines? Were you changing engines out on the salt?

ALEX: We changed engines in back of the Western Motel. They had a little hoist out in back, and we just whipped 'em in and out.

TOM: I've got a picture of Tom Beatty in front of his motel room, and there's a stack of flathead blocks a mile high! He went through those things, like he was goin' through graham crackers. Remember those little cabins behind the Western Motel in Wendover, where Earl Evans and Cobbs and all those guys used to stay?

ALEX: Oh yeah. Well, that's where we stayed first.

TOM: There were engines on the tables!

ALEX: I remember when Ray Brown was sleeping in our cabin, and we woke up in the middle of the night and we thought something was on fire. And he was welding his headers on the floor in the cabin!
Now those were the original cabins. When we knew we were going to go up there in '49 (the first time), we called up the Western Motel and they said, "Well, would you like to stay where Cobb's crew is staying?"
We said, "Oh, yeah, sure, that'd be neat."

So, when we got there, they were staying out in the back in those old wooden cabins. We never stayed out there again! The guys were working on stuff out there all night.

TOM: Earl Evans, Spade Carrillo and all their guys, had the engines apart on the floor and the breakfast table. It was awful! Parts laid out on the bed. Man, it was wild!

ALEX: But, you know, the thing that gets me now is that to us it was very technical, and very serious. I mean, we knew what we were doin'.

The camera captured a typical SCTA starting line scene at an El Mirage dry lake meet during the 1948 season. Identification of #225 is uncertain, but it could be Bill Braun of the Gear Grinders. If so, the car turned 122.95 mph.

But when you think of how simple that engine was, compared with the overhead engines today. I mean, it was such a simple engine. It's amazing that with everybody running virtually the same thing, there could be one guy that went faster than another guy. Because we were all running pretty much the same. I mean what can you do to a flathead? Port and relieve it a little bit.

TOM: I have some pictures of Spalding's modified, that they ran before the war. And it had milled and filled heads, and nothing much else special. And it still ran 130 mph! That was back in 1938! Edelbrock helped you with the engines, right?

ALEX: Vic Edelbrock Sr. helped us a lot. The V8 60 was mine. The B engine was Clyde's, that we built at the speed shop. And the big engine was an Edelbrock engine, and was the same one that we ran in the streamliner at Daytona when we wrecked it. That was the one Bobby Meeks worked on. Bobby went with us.
I ran the V8 60 belly tank, the gold and white one. That was in '48.

In '49 we ran the streamliner. In '50 we ran the streamliner. In January and February of '51 we were invited by Bill France to run the streamliner at Daytona Beach. I asked Ed Winfield, "How much difference do you think there'll be running at 3000 feet at Bonneville, and at sea level?"

He figured it up and said, "Maybe 10% or 15% more horsepower."

So we thought we might have a chance to break that class C international record. The international record at the time was 219 mph, and we got 211 at Bonneville. They told us how wonderful the sand was, that it was hard and smooth. We got down there and it was awful, and the wind was blowin' off the ocean.

So anyhow, after we crashed the car in February of '51...I'm not sure I even ran again in '51. I ran the coupe later, however.

When Hot Rod Magazine ran the coupe, it had a high top so I put a mighty chop job on it. This was a '34. I built the coupe after I stopped running the belly tank with Clyde. But it ended up running a blown Ardun, this car set the record at Pamona dragstrip, 132 something. The record had been 124 mph. And we held that with a blown flathead in that same car. But then a guy came in the speed shop one day and said he had some Ardun heads...would I be interested. Brand new, had never been out of the box. I had 'em on the counter, and I didn't tell anybody...you never know, somebody might steal 'em. They were brand new, had never been touched. They were right from the factory.

TOM: Who was driving this car then?

ALEX: I was driving it when I set the record. But, remember Dave Dalenkin? He was part of a team. He was hanging around the speed shop, and he was driving the car. He kept telling me, "You're not winding it up fast enough in second gear."

What I'd do is, I'd go out strong in second and I'd just pop it in high and let it pull. So he wound the heck out of it in second gear, and when he punched it, it exploded. It caught fire. It was a tragedy. So that was it. I just stopped racing right there.

I sold the coupe to the guys that ran the Pamona dragstrip. They ran it at Bonneville and called it "Miss 400" for a couple of years. It was painted blue and red or something. And I sold the engine, the Ardun, without the blower to some other guys. And they went out to the first Nationals in '55 and won their class. Now, Jim Travis owns the coupe, and he runs it at Bonneville every year.

The number on the streamliner in '49 was #5, but in 1950 it was changed to #2. This was after we redesigned the nose, following Bonneville. The nose came almost straight off. It wasn't designed properly the first time. So we brought it home, and re-did the front. It used to come off very blunt, and now it was more streamlined.

I tried to follow the SCTA rules when I ran my coupe at the lakes, about having the 7" for the windshield stuff. But then I looked at Pierson's coupe. I took it back home and chopped the heck out of it.

Dave Dalenkin bought the tank. Then Dave went to Korea and he sold it to Clyde, and that's how come Clyde and I started running together. It was a B class flathead. It was a record holder. Everyone of those flathead engines ran Edelbrock and Kong equipment. Most of 'em have Winfield cams in 'em, also.

TOM: What ever possessed you to get in to the speed shop business?

ALEX: I don't know. During the service I missed hot rodding so much, I just had that feeling that maybe this would be a good business. You know I used to get Karl and Veda Orr's newsletter, in the mail, and I kind of got excited about it. As it turned out, it was a good decision. I've met a lot of great people over the years because of my participation in the hot rod sport.

The So-Cal Special, freshly painted with the Hot Rod Magazine logo, poses for press photos prior to being towed all the way to Daytona Beach, Florida by Alex Xydias and crew. The So-Cal 'liner and two other hot rods (Ak Miller's Taylor/Ryan modified roadster, and Earl Evans 158-mph tank driven by George Bentley) all went to Florida to run on the beach during the 1951 Speed Week.

Below-This is the original So-Cal Speed Shop as it appeared on Victory Blvd., Burbank, California right after the war. The building was bought from Sears as a pre-fab package. Alex went on to become a very successful speed shop operator.

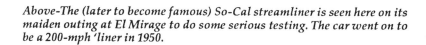

Above-The (later to become famous) So-Cal streamliner is seen here on its maiden outing at El Mirage to do some serious testing. The car went on to be a 200-mph 'liner in 1950.

Alex Xydias and Bill Dailey check with driver Dean Batchelor during an early 1949 lakes meet. The streamliner later got airborne with Dean at the controls, but he walked away okay. The rebuilt car went on to be the 1950 Bonneville C streamliner record holder with a 2-way average speed of 208.9271 mph.

The So-Cal lakester, driven by Alex Xydias, brought home two class records from the 1952 Bonneville National meet. The A lakester record was captured with a 2-way average speed of 152.43 mph and then recorded a 181.085 mph 2-way run to nail down the B lakester record.

With two class records in their possession, the So-Cal crew also was awarded the best appearing car and crew trophy. Here's the crew with all the gold. Left to right: Dailey, Kuns, Sturdy, Xydias and Baldwin. All in all, a very successful Bonneville for this popular crew.

The Baldwin/Barker V8 60-powered A modified roadster running on a local dragstrip. This roadster turned 122.95 mph at the 1st SCTA meet of 1951.

The So-Cal racing team '34 chopped coupe ran both the drags and Bonneville. Runs at the drags, shown here at Pomona under the Xydias/Fox banner in the B modified class, was the record holder in 1954 at 121.16 mph.

The coupe was set for the 1953 Bonneville event and the So-Cal team wanted the C class record. They installed the Fox and Cobb blown 258 cu.in. engine, jumping them a class, and set a 2-way record of 172.749 mph.

Below-So-Cal Speed Shop's '32 3-window coupe off and running at El Mirage on one of its many 120 mph runs.

The mighty red and white So-Cal coupe is pictured here coming off the line at Pomona dragstrip in 1954. Running sans blower, the coupe blasted down the course to a strip record of 121.16 mph — 15 mph faster than the nearest competitor.

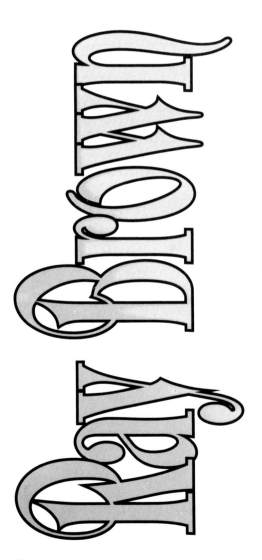

TOM: How did you get interested in roadsters and going to the lakes?

RAY: When I was going to high school (Hollywood High) I was driving around in Culver City one day in my first car, which was a '34 three-window, and I saw some '32 roadsters sitting in front of a drive-in. Something just flashed through my mind that that's what I had to have.

The three years that I was going to high school, I was working for Eddie Meyer Engineering and parking cars at the Florentine Gardens, which was right next door to the Hot Rod Magazine offices in the '50s. That was my life and my hobby. We built mostly V8 60 equipment — heads, manifolds, ran a lot of boats and midgets, and also flathead stuff. I did machine work, porting and relieving work, engine building.

I met Bob Petersen up at the lakes. Then in about 1948, he came over and told to me he was starting up a hot rod magazine.

I was getting more involved, and I got my '32 roadster in pieces and parts, put it together and built a new engine for it. I started running it in 1945. My first run was at a Russetta meet and I did 121.45 mph.

Then I joined up with the Road Runners. I ran the roadster for 2 or 3 years, then I built the mid-engine V8 60, and I built a '27 T and started running that.

Shortly after I started running that with Meyer equipment, I left Eddie Meyer and opened my own shop on Western Avenue. I switched to Evans equipment and ran that for 2 or 3 years, both lakes and Bonneville. I built an engine for Mal Hooper for his roadster, which he ran at lakes. Mal got the idea to build a streamliner, and asked if I wanted to get in on a partnership with him. I had to say no, I couldn't afford it.

After the '27 T, I bought the belly tank for $275 without an engine, and that was a great tank. I put the flathead in it. Then later in 1951 or '52 when Chrysler came out with the new hemispherical engine, I had done a lot of reading and knew that I could get a lot more horsepower out of that than I could with a flathead engine. I called the Chrysler dealer in Culver City and they had 2 of the new engines sitting on the floor. I bought the two identical engines and put one in the belly tank, and ran it for a season or so.

We were getting ready for the streamliner. It was already under construction by Mal Hooper. We knew we were going to run International Class C, so we had to be less than 305 cu. in. So I had to take that 331 inch Chrysler and destroke it and debore it, down to 302 inches. I put in a Herbert roller tappet and cam and ran it in the tank. Our top time in the lakes with the flathead in the tank was 180 mph. Then when we were getting ready for Bonneville we slipped in the Chrysler engine and we hit 201. So we picked up 21 mph. That's when Alex Xydias and I had it out! Those were the last days of the flathead. They got the top time going one way of 198 mph, and I got the two-way record of 201 or 203.

Then in 1952 we brought out the streamliner, and had that same engine in it. That was the same engine we put in Harold White's car (#43), the old Tom Spalding track car. It ran CRA for a few races with a lot of success. We ran the streamliner until 1954. Mal Hooper drove it through the first couple of years, and then Bob Owen drove it in '53 and '54. The top time we got was 250/280 two-way.

We ran it three years. The first year was 231 mph, the second year was 236 mph, and the following year we ran the International meet and we got the 250/280. We ran both Bonneville SCTA and the FIA the week after. That was about the end of it.

I started Bonneville in 1950 and went through 1954. I remember when I was towing the streamliner to Bonneville one year, and the lights were constantly going out. They'd be on for 5 minutes and out they'd go again. It was unbelievable trying to bring that thing to a stop without hitting some cattle or running into someone. So I finally decided to hot wire it right to the battery. I just wrapped it around and put the clamp back on and just let it burn. But it kept the lights on most of the way until dawn came. The next year I bought a brand new truck, so I wouldn't have that problem again. And in the middle of the night on the way to Bonneville, my lights went out on that brand new truck!

The first year that I was going to run the Chrysler engine at Bonneville, I was trying to keep it all under wraps. Stu Hilborn called me up and said he heard I was getting the Chrysler engine ready for Bonneville. He asked if he could come up and take some dimensions to make injectors. So Stu came up and sat on the floor of my shop for a couple of hours and degreed out everything and made the original layouts for his injectors for the Chrysler engine.

TOM: What did you pay for those two new Chrysler engines?

RAY: A little over $700 apiece, complete. It was the biggest, heaviest thing I ever saw. The heads didn't flow well at all. The following year you could get the marine heads with the large valves and large ports and that improved it considerably. It was a good stout engine though. You really couldn't hurt it too much. It was so much fun doing development work on a hemispherical engine after all those years of flatheads. Bobby Meeks told me what Vic Edelbrock said the first year we brought it out. His tank was running 200, right? All of a sudden we beat him by a couple of miles an hour; did it on alcohol. Bobby and Vic said, "This is going to be the end of an era."

In 1950 I brought out the first automobile seatbelts. In those days, I was buying used 3-inch military stuff. I'd disassemble and rebuild 'em and polish and plate 'em. I got new webbing, and got some floor hardware so they could be run in cars. I ran ads in Hot Rod Magazine in '50 and all the way through. In 1954, the seatbelt business got much larger and got to be much more rewarding. I was in business from 1950 - 1966.

TOM: Did Superior Industries buy you out?

RAY: I sold out to American Safety. Lou Borick at Superior Industries

Harold White, an employee of Ray Brown Automotive, at the wheel of his '25 T roadster pictured here at Paradise Mesa drag strip near San Diego, California. Ray offers last minute instructions. A 119 mph 1/4-mile speed was recorded with a Ford V8 flat motor.

was a good friend of mine. He went in the seatbelt business shortly after I did. After I sold out to American Safety, I had to stay with them for about 16 months on a contract. When my tenure was up, I retired at age 39. I retired from the business, but I was still thinking hot rods, but not really wanting to go back into the manufacturing business again.

Then Lou Borick at Superior Industries called me one day. He was already in the accessory business, but wanted to go in the wheel business. I hadn't had any wheel experience, but from there we started. Mostly in the aftermarket for the first year or two, but then in 1970 when Carroll Shelby's operation on the west coast was closed up, there was a fellow by the name of Tim Foreacre who was on the scene with Borick. He had worked for Carroll Shelby and had made an arrangement with Ford Motor Company to move back to Detroit and to have a parts location available for Ford vehicles. He wanted to put aluminum wheels on it, so he gave us a tooling order and we put out a couple hundred wheels or so. I was back in Detroit at the time, and came to make the delivery. He told me that Ford was going to close down that distribution center completely. He said, "I'll let you have the tooling back if you want, at10 cents on the dollar, and you can keep the wheels or I'll pay you for them."

That very day in 1970, at about 4 degrees above zero (and no gloves), I took two of those wheels and looked for some Ford building. The taxi driver said, "You must be from L.A." Three years later in 1973 I took a production order for cast aluminum wheels for the 1974 Ford Mustang. It was the first year they used cast aluminum wheels. Did the same thing for GM in 1976. I got the tooling order for their first cast aluminum

wheels for the 1977 Cutlass. I went over to Chrysler and we got some truck business, and we made the first cast aluminum wheels for their '79 pickup trucks.

TOM: You were assistant starter on the board for SCTA?

RAY: I was starter one year. And I was president of the SCTA in 1953, I believe. I've got the gavel.

The Golden Years in hot rodding were after the war from about '45 to '55. Then after the drags came out, it all changed. Some guys went into it, some didn't. I didn't care for the drags. I put my engine in Micky Thompson's dragster, and we were the first dragster to run faster than 150 mph.

One thing most people don't realize is that when Hot Rod Magazine started out, there wasn't any drag racing, it was all lakes or street and circle track.

I've got the first issues when Wally Parks started talking about that. Somebody wrote in and said, "How come we don't have a national association?" I remember being with Wally when he said he was going to move down the street to set up the National Hot Rod Association.

Alex Xydias was a good buddy of mine, and I was always impressed by the fact that he had a speed shop. Then in 1950, when I opened the speed shop on Western and Lemon Grove, that was the first speed shop in Hollywood.

In the years that have gone by since 1954 (and the days that I was in hot rodding), in all those many years that I was in business, I still look back on the racing days as the best days of my life. I haven't forgotten anything about those days. In all the years that have gone by, when I try to think of something that I really enjoyed...those were the days!

Hot rodders found this famous race car in one of the service stations in Wendover and had to roll it out for some photos. The car is the world famous Mormon Meteor driven by Ab Jenkins, pioneer hot rodder. Some of Ab's records (world and American) set on the Bonneville salt are 100 miles at 196.35 mph average, 200 miles at 195.85 mph average, 1000 miles at 172.804 mph average, and 1 hour at 195.95 mph average. Not too shabby!

Ray Brown's rear-engine dry lakes car showing the V8-60 rear-engine set-up. The engine is mounted to allow it to pivot in the frame. Tranny is a Sower in and out dog clutch. Cooling is supplied by a front-mounted radiator with water being flowed back and forth by aluminum tubes. Car turned 134.73 mph in 1949 SCTA meet.

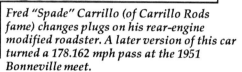

Fred "Spade" Carrillo (of Carrillo Rods fame) changes plugs on his rear-engine modified roadster. A later version of this car turned a 178.162 mph pass at the 1951 Bonneville meet.

Right- A very nice looking channeled '32 lakes roadster gets ready to make a pass down the course during a 1947 SCTA lakes meet.

The Burke-Francisco belly tank "world's fastest hot rod", with the fastest one-way time ever recorded at a SCTA dry lakes meet. Driven by Bill Phy, June 1949 at a speed of 164.83 mph.

Vic Edelbrock Sr. waits in line with his mighty '32 roadster. Vic was a top runner in this car before the war. Most all of his early speed equipment was race tested with this fine roadster. Vic belonged to the Road Runners club.

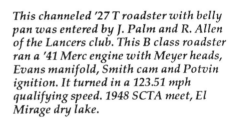

This channeled '27 T roadster with belly pan was entered by J. Palm and R. Allen of the Lancers club. This B class roadster ran a '41 Merc engine with Meyer heads, Evans manifold, Smith cam and Potvin ignition. It turned in a 123.51 mph qualifying speed. 1948 SCTA meet, El Mirage dry lake.

Glendale Strokers club member Tom Beatty recorded a 129.68 mph speed in this B class roadster in 1948. Engine was a 21-stud 1932 Ford engine equipped with Navarro heads and manifold, Weber cam and his own ignition.

Frank Breen, Road Runner club member, checks the plugs on the Breen and Haller B class streamliner belly tank. The Evans equipped '40 Merc ran 127.65 mph at a 1948 SCTA meet on El Mirage dry lake bed.

Ray Brown at the wheel of his sharp looking '32 roadster at a 1947 SCTA lakes meet. Ray's C class roadster ran a full Eddie Meyer equipped Merc engine, recording a time of 123.62 mph on September 21, 1947.

Roadster City USA! This is how it looked on the early morning starting line at El Mirage dry lake in 1947. It was the early bird who got to run first.

This 1948 Road Runner club picture displays nearly all the cars that were in competition that year. The Road Runners were the club point winner for '48, finishing with the highest point total of the 23 SCTA clubs.

This was a special engine developed and built by Ray Brown Automotive for an east coast customer. Check that wild looking 4-carburetor set-up.

1948's fastest roadster clocked by SCTA at 148.27 mph one way with a two-way average of 138.975 mph. Owned and built by Regg Schlemmer, this black and yellow beauty ran a full belly pan, 268 cu.in. Merc engine, Evans heads and manifold, Smith & Jones cam, and a dual Wico magneto. Rearend gear was 3.27:1, tires were 750x16, turning the engine 5700 rpm on akly during the record 148 mph run.

Ray Brown, as a boy, talking with Bud Meyer regarding the V8-60 engine in Bud's 135 Hydro racing boat. During the '48-'49 season, this boat was one of the top contenders in its class. Ray was working at Eddie Meyers' shop at this time.

With the help of Red Wilson and Tony Capanna, one of Ray Brown's flathead engines is given the supreme test on Tony's Wilcap dyno to see how much horsepower it would produce on straight methanol. Result was 218 hp, which was the most hp any flathead had developed for that time — 1947-'48. This engine ran 201 mph in Ray's belly tank later in the season.

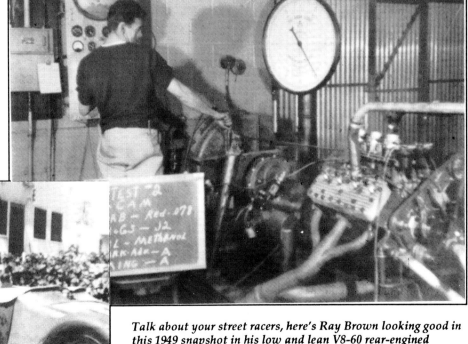

Talk about your street racers, here's Ray Brown looking good in this 1949 snapshot in his low and lean V8-60 rear-engined roadster. Ray looks like he just ran 140 right in his Hollywood, California driveway.

How about a 106 mph pass in a '34 Ford convert? Ray Brown strikes a hero pose after a quick run in Danny O'Shea's '34 on April 18, 1946 at a Russetta meet.

Ray Brown and crew of his #99 C class roadster. Picture was snapped at a SCTA El Mirage lakes meet September 21, 1947. Best speed was 123.62 mph.

A run of 134.73 mph was recorded by this '27 T rear-engine A class roadster at a June 1949 SCTA meet. Owned and driven by Ray Brown, the 1938 Ford V8-60 engine was bored and stroked. It ran Evans 8.75:1 heads and a 2-carb Evans intake manifold, Harmon and Collins cam, and Kong ignition.

SCTA meet, June 1950 saw Ray Brown's little V8-60 powered roadster on the line sporting a new nose and hood. On this day, Ray ran 137.40 mph one way, but failed to break the two-way record. The 156 cu.in. V8-60 engine with Evans heads and manifold, Smith cam and Kong ignition did, however, become the 1950 Bonneville class A lakester record holder with a 134.120 mph two-way average.

This sharp looking '25 T track roadster, owned by the White Brothers, is shown here running the 302 cu.in. de-stroked Chrysler hemi engine that ran 251 mph in the Shadoff Special streamliner at Bonneville. The car ran the CRA circuit for two seasons and gave the flathead V8 boys fits.

Burning the midnight oil at Ray Brown's shop prior to a lakes meet. Ray (lower foreground), and Don Francisco, Hot Rod Magazine tech editor, discuss engine specs of the 180 mph tank engine. Ray's V8-60 rear-motored roadster gets plenty of attention from two of Ray's crew.

Johnny Johnson in the Johnson-Caruthers B streamliner record holder, with a two-way average speed of 139.39 mph. Merc engine was fitted with Edelbrock heads and manifold, Winfield cam and Edelbrock ignition. Record was set October 19, 1947 at El Mirage dry lake SCTA meet.

Bob Bowen sits atop the Shadoff Special C class streamliner after losing a right front tire tread on his 252 mph return run during the 1953 Bonneville National. Ray Brown built the powerful Chrysler hemi V8 engine.

The car and crew of the 1953 international record holding Shadoff Special C class streamliner. The Shadoff liner was designed by Dean Bachelor, engineered by Carl Fleischmann, constructed and driven by Mal Hooper. Chrysler hemi V8 engine was built by Ray Brown of Ray Brown Automotive in Los Angeles. Sponsorship was by Bill Shadoff, a Pomona Chrylser dealer. Crew (L to R): Karl Fleischmann, Bill Shadoff, Ray Brown, Robert Taylor, Mal Hooper and Herb Francis.

One of Ray Brown's shop crew, Bob Rodick, in his '32 C class Ford roadster that Bob ran at the lakes in 1947.

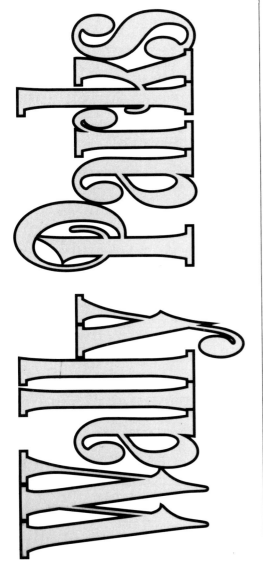

TOM: Do you know when guys first started running the lakes?

WALLY: I don't know when they started, but Muroc timing was the Purdy brothers. They were probably the first organized group up there, although there were other kinds of races there that involved AAA cars, but they were usually into the individual record run. There was Bell Timing, Mojave Timing, Russetta of course.

TOM: Russetta came along right after the war due to the fact that SCTA wouldn't let you run coupes and stuff.

WALLY: That was the main motivation. It was a group of guys, Baney and Pearson and that bunch, who wanted to run coupes. Their timer was Raymond who had his own timer. SCTA was using Otto Crocker. It started out as kind of an off-shoot renegade group to do the same thing that SCTA did only to concentrate on allowing coupes and sedan-like cars to run.

TOM: When did SCTA start letting coupes and sedans run?

WALLY: It wasn't a rivalry situation. It just made sense. I think maybe there was a limit on the number of available open-body cars then. Maybe there was starting to be a decline of roadsters. I don't really recall the circumstances. Eventually SCTA probably decided it wasn't good to let somebody else have some of the business.

What used to impress me was when guys would come up with current year model cars with the fenders stripped off, and take 'em out and run the doggone things. They were so beautiful.

When the Muroc Timing Association was running, and I think in the early days of SCTA, the common practice was to go out and qualify. You either qualify in a 70-80 mph hour class, or the 80-90 class, or 90-100, or100 and over. Then whatever class you qualified in, they ran off the class eliminations. They'd just line up across the lake bed and have at it. Six or eight cars, or whatever.

They'd line up and a pace car would run alongside 'em way out at the edge of the course. And there'd be a flagman, hanging onto the side of the pace car. When he saw that the cars were reasonably lined up and going at a good enough speed, he'd wave the flag and everybody would go. One of the best flaggers was Francis Luehm.

The first days I ran up there, I drove Jack Henry's roadster. And we qualified at 83 mph, in the 80-90 mph class. I was running a Chevy 4. This was our first time out running the thing. But anyway, it came time for the race and we were in the 80-90 mph class.

We took off in this long line of cars, and the flagman was hanging on the side of the pace car. And when he gave us the flag, we got on it. Fortunately the combination on this roadster of Jack Henry's, was a good engine. It took off and I was able to kind of be out in front, along with a couple of others that I could see kind of out the corner of my eye. In back, there was nothing but a giant dustbowl. I stayed on it goin' toward the finish line, really cookin', dust and more dust. It seemed like you ran forever. I think they ran a three mile course at that time. They timed 'em with a great big piano wire stretched across the course about six inches above the surface, that triggered a mechanical thing. It worked a stop watch.

So, I'm driving and driving and driving, and I can see these cars off to the left. Finally, I'm lookin' and waitin' and waitin' for the time trap to come up, and tryin' to keep an eye on who's out there tryin' to come past me. Finally this trip wire came up, and I knew that was the end of the trap. So I crossed it and backed off, and everybody flew past me. Then I realized, too late, that I had cut it off at the first wire. So, I tried to get back into it, and back in the dust you could see nothing, absolutely nothing.

So, I didn't dare back off, I didn't dare go fast, I just sat there and prayed. Finally, as people slowed down ahead, I could kind of find a chance to edge off to the side and pull out of it. It was very dangerous, particularly for anybody who wasn't in the front row. We lost five racers the hard way.

TOM: When did they finally stop running it like that?

WALLY: I don't know what the years were. SCTA decided they had to put a limit on the number of cars that could run. So they cut it back to four cars running abreast for the finals, or the run-offs. Then, later on they were becoming more safety conscious, they put the limit back to two abreast. And it was still a problem, because the lake beds were sometimes not in the greatest condition. They ultimately went to just one car at a time. It continued that way from that time on. But it was dangerous. The only thing that was any more dangerous than running in the races, was getting to and from this place. On those roads going in, everybody was running flat out.

TOM: When was the first time you went to the lakes?

147

WALLY: I was just getting out of high school in the early '30s. The first tag time I got up there on my own was 1933. And I think the first time I went up to see the lakes, I went up with some friends of mine in about 1928. That's when it was run what ya' brung. And everybody was out there runnin'.

They were running the lakes in the late '20s, and some of 'em were pretty well organized. As they started attracting a lot of people, it became tougher to run. I think George Wight was the proprieter of Muroc Timing Association. He was one of the spearheads of the thing. I think Bell Auto Parts probably was the sponsor of the organized races that they put on. And then the SCTA kind of filled the gap.

TOM: When did guys start the SCTA?

WALLY: The first meeting of the SCTA was on November 29, 1937. At that time, the initial clubs were the Sidewinders, the Idlers, Ninety Mile An Hour Club, the Ramblers, the Throttlers, the Road Runners, and the Night Riders. Ed Adams, who was a memeber of the Night Riders, was the first elected President of the SCTA. Another prominent name was Art Tilton. He was secretary and one of the strongest leaders of the organization. The first chairman was Verne Hurst.

TOM: You drove a tank called Sweet Sixteen, didn't you?

WALLY: Yeah, that was the Burke and Francisco tank. It had Model T frame rails. Somewhere along the line Burke had cut a couple of notches out of the frame rail. So, we made our first run with it. Just about a quarter of a mile off the starting line, I noticed that the steering wheel had changed positions. But, I found out I could still steer it, so I got back into the thing and took off again. I got out a little way, and all of a sudden it changed position again, the other way. But I could still steer it, so I got back in and went again and made the run. We were doin' 139 mph and it was just like a half pass. So at the end of the run, I took the car back to see what it was. The frame rail had broken in two and it was layin' down in the bottom of the tank, and it was the axles shifting back and forth.

Francisco and I knew that the thing would really run, if we gave it another chance. We wanted to be the first ones to hit 150 mph at the lakes. Nobody had gone that fast yet. So, we tried to talk Burke into taking it into town and welding it up, but Burke had to go home that night. He promised he'd be back Saturday night.

So, we ended up with kind of a split-up in the team, Burke loaded the car on the trailer and took it on back into town. And in the meantime, while we were arguing, Howard Wilson went out and turned 150 mph in Stu Hilborn's car.

As I look back on those early lakes days, I have to admit they were something special. It was fun!

Left-Doug Hartlet, member of the SCTA Lancers club, turned 134.93 mph in his "B" roadster in 1948 running a '46 Merc engine, Evans heads and manifold, Clay Smith cam and Potvin ignition.

Bottom Left- Norm Lean, one ot the Dolphins club top competitors, turned 121.45 mph at a 1948 SCTA meet with his '32 "B" roadster. The '46 Merc engine ran Navarro heads and manifold, Emery cam and his own special ignition.

Below-Stroker club member Harold Osborn slipped his "C" class '29 roadster through the SCTA lights for a time of 122.61 mph at El Mirage in 1948. The '46 Merc engine was equipped with Edelbrock heads and manifold, Smith cam and Spalding ignition.

Ray Brown, Road Runner member, gets ready for a quick pass in his new V8-60 powered, rear-engined '27 T roadster. Ray built the car while employed at Eddie Meyer Engineering Company. Photo taken at El Mirage dry lake in 1948.

Strokers club member Art Tremaine and his '29 Ford "B" roadster turned 115.83 mph at a 1948 SCTA meet. Powered by a '46 Merc flathead with Edmunds heads, Navarro manifold, Smith cam and Potvin ignition.

Here's the famous Paul Schiefer, of San Diego Flywheel & Clutch Mfg., waiting in line in his '32 roadster before the war.

George Harvey's trick modified looks like it has an old Ascot Speedway front end. Powered by a 21-stud Ford V8.

This vintage looking '23 Model T belongs to "Multy" Aldrich. Running Rajo racing equipment, this car ran the 1947 SCTA season as a joint entry with Bill Passer. Both are Hornet club members.

This pre-war streamliner was a head-turner wherever it ran at the lakes. Affectionately known as the "Coca-Cola Stand", it was owned by Jack Harvey.

Who says lakes racing is just a man's sport? These two lovely ladies sure look like they were enjoying the action. Helping out with Don Arnett's (Santa Ana, California) "C" class '32 roadster during a 1948 SCTA meet. Don coaxed a 125.77 mph effort from his '39 Merc engine, equipped with Evans heads and manifold, Smith cam, homebuilt Zephyr ignition. Good for 140 season points.

Road Masters club member Al Eurengy's '32 hiboy roadster. Ford flathead V8 engine was equipped with Offenhauser heads, Navarro manifold, Isky cam.

Above- Jim Harber's 127-mph '27 T V8 roadster set up for both street and lakes. Power supplied by '40 Merc engine, equipped with Edelbrock heads and manifold, Winfield cam and Potvin ignition.

The Throttlers club pit area at an early post-war lakes meet. #419C is Pat O'Briens's '32 roadster. Under the tent, Arnold Birner's 4-port Riley.

This rear-engined 4-port Riley 4-banger ran 141.06 mph in July 1948 at an SCTA meet. Owned and driven by Arnold Birner, a Throttlers club member.

Pat O'Brien's '32 hiboy roadster at speed on El Mirage dry lake August 1948. This run netted Pat the fastest drive-up car time of '48. 115.83 mph on gas engine, '41 Merc 3-5/16" bore, 3-7/8" stroke. Ford heads, Edelbrock slingshot manifold, Kurten ignition, and Winfield cam. Car has column shift, '40 Zephyr gears, '34 Ford 3.54:1 rear end gear. Driven to and from work, placed 3rd in the '48 Pasadena Roadster Club's reliability run. Pat belonged to the Throttlers club.

This class "B" channeled '32 roadster turned 109.79 mph running a 21-stud flatmotor equipped with Meyers heads, Thickston manifold, Winfield cam and a special ignition built by Ted Peckles, owner and driver.

Right- The Jeraulds Speed Shop entry out of National City, California entered by Barbe and Dalph. This full-belly-panned '25 T "C" class roadster turned 133 mph running Offenhauser heads and manifold and a Barker mag.

Harvey Haller (right) and Frank Breen, winners of the 1948 Pasadena Roadster Club's second annual reliability run are pictured here with Harvey's winning roadster.

Below- Colleen Townsend, movie actress, tries on Bill Burke's "Sweet Sixteen" belly tank lakester for size. Picture was used to promote the first hot rod show held in Los Angeles, California from January 23 - 25, 1948.

Frank Leonard's Channeled "B" class T roadster. This neat little Evans equipped roadster turned 143.31 mph at the November 1948 Russetta meet at El Mirage dry lake bed.

Dick Kraft, member of the SCTA Lancers club, in his 130.34 mph T roadster streamliner in 1947.

The channeled '34 roadster lurking behind the DeSoto grille and chopped '46 Ford radiator belonged to Don Cox, member of the Carlsbad Oilers. The engine room is filled with a 59A block, bored .030 over, Merc 9.5:1 Evans heads, Cannon cam, Weiand manifold and a stock 21-A Ford ignition. Turned 113.63 mph @ 5350 rpm on pump gas.

Road Master club member Harold Johansen's "B" class T roadster turned 118.57 mph with a Riley OHV set-up for a Merc flathead engine. He ran his own manifold, Ford ignition and Riley cam.

Unidentified driver (possibly "Bunkey") poses for this photo in his bobtailed T roadster. From the looks of the headlights and front bumper, it was driven on the street.

Below- Bill Jenks (Santa Ana, California) up in his '32 Ford roadster. This 260 cu.in. "C" roadster turned 118.73 mph running Evans heads and manifolds, Bertrand cam and Arnette ignition.

This Riley 4-port-powered '27 T roadster turned 109.75 mph. Owned by Jack Thompson, Road Master club member.

Henry L. Simbro's "B" roadster turned 107.65 mph running a '34 Ford V8 engine with Edmunds heads, Weiand manifold, Winfield cam and Mal Ord ignition. Henry belonged to the Road Masters.

A popular stop for a lot of the homeward bound lakes boys was the Union station in Palmdale. Jimmy Khougaz #707C channeled '32 and Harold Johanson's T, complete with lake dust, pause before heading for LA.

Below- Jim Scott's '32 hiboy roadster waiting in line at a post-war SCTA meet. His "B" class roadster turned 108.13 mph.

This streetable '34 Ford roadster ran 118.84 mph in "B" class, SCTA clocks. The '41 Merc engine ran Navarro heads and manifold, Harmon & Collins cam, and Arnette ignition. Owned by Alan Crain.

Orange, California resident Vic Schnackenberg's pretty green roadster shows off its trick interior and dash. Car turned 122.61 mph at the April '48 SCTA meet. Note the '40 column shift set-up.

This fine looking '29 roadster on '32 rails belongs to Bill Roberts. Power is supplied by flathead Ford V8, equipped with a set of Riley OHV heads. "Deni" at the wheel.

Gene Bowman's '32 roadster clocked 117.63 mph at a 1947 SCTA lakes meet. Engine ran 3/8" bore, Meyers heads, Weiand manifold and a Harmon & Collins cam.

This '27 T modified ran a 4-cylinder Cragar head set-up. Car belonged to Road Master club member Jack Rigby.

Bozzy Willis, San Diego, California lakes enthusiast in his "Steam Beans" modified. Bozzy could always be seen at the lakes with his mighty Bolex 16mm color movie camera recording early lakes history.

Randy Shinn of Pasadena, California was the 1946 SCTA roadster record holder with a speed of 128.66 mph. The car was also run on the streets.

Jimmy Khougaz's "C" class channeled '32 roadster. Engine is '46 Merc with Offenhauser heads, Weiand manifold, Winfield cam and Henry ignition. Ran 123.28 mph on the SCTA clocks.

The "Pride of Long Beach", the Daighs Special. This "C" class roadster was run by Chuck and Harold Daigh, a slightly over 250 cu.in. "C" engine against all the big-bore, long-strokers, and still gave them what for! It was one of the first 125-mph cars at the beginning of the 1948 season.

This class "C" roadster record holder was run by Don "Nog" McLean, member of the San Diego Roadster club. Check that "four of a kind" on his 1949 California license plate.

One of the early front-engine belly tanks running at the lakes right after WWII. The "D" behind the number means that's a very large flatmotor, or the lettering man was out to lunch.

Frank Breen, ready to go in his "B" streamliner belly tank. Rear-engine '40 Merc ran Evans heads and manifold, Weber cam, his own ignition. Turned 127.65 mph SCTA, 1948.

Unidentified OHV head set-up mounted on a Ford flathead V8. Lake racers would go to any lengths to go a little faster.

Mickey Thompson's wife (left) and her girlfriend do some wrenching in between runs at an early post-war Russetta meet.

A typical 1948 SCTA starting line scene. The new automatic starting lights were used for the first time at the April '48 event. Cars came off the line every 20 seconds. System was originated by Kong Jackson of the Glendale Sidewinders.

Lou Baney, on the phone, gets a good looking '29 roadster on its way to the lights during an October 1950 Russetta meet.

A typical El Mirage dry lake scene during the SCTA 1950 season. Those were the days!

Fine looking '32 lakes roadster, complete with full race tarp, open header pipe and split wishbone to make clearance for the low slung engine oil pan.

A pre-war rear-engine full belly-panned '29 Ford roadster. Note aluminum firewall and "B" class gauges opposite the driver.

Don Francisco with the rear end out of the Burke/Francisco "C" belly tank. This car was the "C" streamliner record holder at 144.855 mph as of the June 1948 SCTA meet.

Above- SCTA V8 60 Ford-powered panel truck provides a backdrop for Harvey Haller's "B" roadster along with an unidentified rear-engine wing tank. El Mirage, 1948.

Above- Gus Maanum, on the crutches, is the artist responsible for all the great action drawings of the famous lakes cars that appeared on SCTA meet programs and in Hot Rod Magazine. Gus lost a leg as the result of a hit-and-run motorcycle accident in 1945. Gus captured the lakes scene like no other artist ... he was the best.

Stu Hilborn makes early morning adjustments on his "B" streamliner. Engine is '34 Ford V8. Heads are filled and milled, manifold was designed and built by Eddie Miller. Running 4 carburetors: 3 Stromberg E's and a Double E Stromberg. Turned a 145.640 2-way average. "B" streamliner SCTA record holder.

The Coahran & Downey '29 "B" roadster pickup representing the San Diego Roadsters club. This little jewel turned 114.64 mph running a '46 Merc, Evans heads and manifold, Weber cam and Pounden mag. Ran SCTA during the 1948 season.

1947 "B" roadster record holder, Doug Hartlet, ran a 2-way average of 129.365 mph. Doug, a member of the Lancers, had a qualifying speed in early '48 of 134.93 mph.

Alex Xydias showed up at El Mirage in '48 with this beautiful V8 60-powered "A" class wing tank streamliner. Paint job was a stunning gold and white. The sponsor was, who else, but Alex's own Burbank, California-based So-Cal Speed Shop.

This unidentified super neat '27 T roadster must have been running a LaSalle or Caddy flathead V8 from the looks of the overhead exhaust. Excellent construction, and what a great drive-in car!

This Pasadena-based "B" class '32 roadster was built by Bob Klaeser in 1947. Engine is early '38 Ford block, Spalding cam and ignition, Edelbrock manifold, and Cydine heads. Full pressure fuel system, and 3.78:1 gears. Ran 119.05 mph at the September '48 SCTA meet.

The Burke/Francisco "C" streamliner record holder with a 2-way average speed of 144.85 mph. Body is constructed from a 300-gallon aircraft drop tank. Engine is a 272 cu.in. '42 Merc with a stock stroke and 3/8" overbore. 1948.

Karl Orr's #1 record-holding V8-powered modified. This car held the SCTA modified record for 1942 of 133.03 mph. A member of the Alrata club, Karl was also the 1942 season champion. This car also ran 125 mph with a Cragar, running a stock exhaust system.

Powered by a '39 Ford V8 60, this sleek "A" class tank is owned by Don Lodes of the SCTA Road Runners club. The mighty 60 ran a Weber cam.

Jack Avakian's "Little Red Wagon", a smooth looking rear-engined T roadster was a top class contender during the 1948 SCTA lakes season. Jack's '46 Merc "B" class engine ran special Ford heads, Edelbrock manifold, Smith cam and Spalding ignition. It turned a speed of 128.02 mph.

Paul Schiefer's immaculate '25 T roadster. Paul, a So. California Roadster club member turned 136.77 mph in this little beauty during the 1948 season. Although not shown here, Paul was the first one to run motorcycle front wheels on his roadster at the lakes.

C.W. Scott, better known as "Scotty", and his super looking street & lakes roadster. Check out the windshield treatment. Scotty, a lakes and Bonneville veteran, was a member of the SCTA Hornets club.

Low down and ready, this channeled '29 roadster, running a very custom hood, is waiting its turn to run. Notice the absence of a crash helmet.

This smooth looking '29 roadster from San Bernardino, California was owned by Junior Tucker, member of the San Bernardino Roadster club. The 205 cu.in., 2-port Riley ran 102.68 mph in 1947. How about that Duval type windshield.

Another San Bernardino area roadster running the lakes during the 1948 season was this C class T roadster owned by Bill Harber. The Ford V8 engine equipped with Edelbrock manifold, Offenhauser heads, Winfield cam and Potvin ignition ran 124.99 mph.

Pasadena Roadster club member Leonard M. Koch's B class roadster pickup turned a best 1948 time of 105.38 mph running stock V8 heads, manifold, ignition and Harmon & Collins cam.

Right- Road Masters club member Paul Grousso and his 4-port Riley-powered '29 roadster. Check the tin in the background.

Below right- Wally O'Brien and his C class '32 roadster that he ran during the 1948 SCTA season. Wally ran 125.87 mph with his '41 Merc engine equipped with Evans heads, Weiand manifold, Smith cam and Evans ignition. He was a member of the Strokers club.

Below- Here it is, the "Lakes Monster". It's Charles Dimmitt in his 147-inch wheelbase '39 Zephyr convertible-bodied D class roadster. Running 452 cu.in. 1931 Caddy V16 engine, driving the rearend through two Caddy transmissions (one reversed). Driver sits between the front wheels. Car required 3 years to build and was new for the '48 season.

#540 C class roadster, owned by Bob Bennett, Glendale Sidewinder member, recorded a 121.13 mph speed during the 1948 SCTA season. Engine was a '46 Merc, Navarro heads and manifold, Winfield cam, Kong ignition.

Left- Jim Hoffman's '30 Model A roadster on '32 rails. Custom aluminum 3-piece hood. Engine was a '46 Mercury, Edelbrock equipped.

Oilers club member "Dago" Cantarini's narrowed '27 T-bodied roadster, mounted on Essex rails. Engine, '42 Merc, 3-5/16 bore, 1/8 stroke, Offie heads and manifold, Harmon & Collins cam, Pouden magneto. This slick little T turned 123.28 mph on alky at a 1948 SCTA meet.

Don Jensen, president of the Clutchers Roadster club, getting set to make a 117.96 mph pass at El Mirage during a 1948 SCTA meet.

Rod runs and get togethers were popular back in 1948. Here the Strokers club is shown at Big bear Lake on one of their club outings.

Strokers club member Frank Beagle with his C class '29 roadster. Frank's 128.20 mph roadster ran a '42 Merc engine, Navarro heads, Edelbrock manifold, Smith cam and ignition.

Al Pahland in his '32 roadster waits his turn in line during a 1948 SCTA meet at El Mirage dry lake near Palmdale, California.

The Beatty & Navarro entry with Barney Navarro at the wheel. This 1948 C class roadster ran a '41 Ford V8 engine with Navarro heads, Navarro supercharger set up, Winfield cam and Kurten ignition. The car ran 139+ mph.

This smart looking '27 T roadster ran a 229 cu.in. B class Ford 6 engine. Stock head, Kundsen manifold and Clay Smith cam. It clocked a one-way speed of 117.80 mph. The car belonged to Jim Woods, a member of the Road Runners club.

Nite Owls club members Tham and Greiner entered this 1930 Model A roadster, running a '32 Ford 4-cylinder engine equipped with a Riley 2-port head, Thomas manifold, Winfield cam and Wico mag.

This smooth looking, unidentified, '29 Ford C class roadster lays down a batch of lakes dust as it charges toward the timing lights on El Mirage dry lake bed.

Two fine looking lakes roadsters belonging to Glendale Sidewinders members Dick Sagran (#230c) 125.34 mph, and Bob Taylor (#232c) 120.32. mph.

Johnny Goldman in his 115.97 mph '32 roadster. Engine was full Edelbrock with a Clay Smith cam. Nice looking set-up. Check the roadsters in the background. Picture was shot at Gardena's Carrell Speedway during a 1948 CRA race.

Above- Roadmasters club member Ed Harding's wild looking red streamliner. A 4"x4-1/2" Cragar set-up supplied the ponies.

Above- Here's what a dry lake looks like when it's not dry. This is El Mirage dry lake under water, October 22nd, 1948.

This beautiful '32 roadster was owned by Major Gilbert, Glendale, CA. It ran as a C class roadster at the lakes, running a '46 Merc engine with Navarro heads and manifold, Winfield cam and Kong ignition. Check the neat windshield set-up.

Hot Rod Magazine, Oct. 1948 displayed this fine '32 roadster owned by Bob McGee, on its cover. Car was bright red at the time and was one of the finest examples of roadster craftsmanship to be seen in southern California. Car was built in 1940, ran its first lakes in 1941. This is the car that Dick Scritchfield, LA Roadsters, has owned for many years.

#807b, the "Door Prize roadster". Nelson Morris won this fine '32 roadster at the First Annual Hot Rod Exposition sponsored by the SCTA, 1948 at the L. A. National Guard Armory. Car was built at the show by members of the SCTA and ran 106.38 mph its first lakes meet. Nelson belonged to the Dolphins club.

Road Runner club member Harvey Haller's sharp looking B class roadster. Harvey ran Evans heads, Evans manifold on his V8 Ford engine. It was a top point getter for his club during the 1947 season. Ran 128.57 mph at 1948 SCTA meet.

A Road Runner threesome (left to right) "Old Dad" Miller, Harvey Haller, Ak Miller pose for a snapshot at El Mirage dry lake, 1948.

Wailing up a storm is Gordon Patterson's B class roadster on El Mirage dry lake, running a 239 cu.in. 1940 DeSoto 6. Engine was stock except for homemade intake manifold, Harman & Collins cam and Mallory ignition. 118.11 mph was best time for the '48 season.

Bert Letner's beautiful track and lakes roadster at speed on El Mirage dry lake in 1948. Bert's red and white roadster turned a 130.05 mph at a Pacific Timing Association meet. In its first track outing at Carrell Speedway, it was quick qualifier and was off the track record by only 5/100ths of a second. Bert belonged to the Road Runners.

Ed (Axle) Stewart's very clean '32 C class roadster. A member of the San Diego Roadster club, Ed is the originator of the "Dago" dropped Ford front axle. Ed's Merc engine ran Cyclone heads and Evans manifold.

San Diego's own Paul Schiefer in his outstanding C class T roadster. The workmanship on this car was out of sight. Paul loved to come up from the border city and give the L.A. boys fits both at the lakes and on the street.

Right- This Pasadena, California-based '29 roadster ran a 1939 6-cylinder .030-over Chevrolet engine, stock head, special manifold, and Harmon & Collins full-race cam. Car was owned by Bill Vander Ploeg of Pasadena, California. Best 1947 lakes time was 105.05 mph.

Left- The Beam and Noble B class '29 Ford pickup was powered by a Merc engine with Cyclone heads and manifold, Smith cam, Potvin ignition, and had a 3.78:1 rearend gear. Best 1947-'48 time was 119.99 mph (sideways).

The Coshow Brothers '29 on '32 rails. This fine looking lakes roadster from Long Beach, California turned a quick 133.33 mph at a 1948 SCTA meet at El Mirage under the Lancer club banner. Engine was a '39 Merc with Weiand heads, Navarro manifold, Smith cam and Potvin ignition.

The Alger and Starr B class roadster from Brea, California turned 132.74 mph speed during a 1948 SCTA El Mirage lake meet. The 1941 Mercury engine was equipped with Earl Evans heads and manifold, a Smith 272 cam and Potvin ignition. A very strong runner.

#736 B roadster was owned and run by Tommy Dahm of Pasadena, California during the 1948 SCTA season. The '29 A body on '32 frame ran a 1938 Ford V8 engine of 244 cu.in. displacement. At the July '48 meet it clocked 122.11 mph for its best time.

The Lou Baily and Ray Bingham B class roadster smoked through the SCTA lights for a speed of 123.45 mph on El Mirage dry lake bed in 1948. The Gear Grinders is their club.

A beautiful unidentified sprint car that showed up at El Mirage dry lake bed to do battle with the SCTA clocks. A very nicely constructed car for the period. Love those louvers!

Don Conroy's B class '29 on '32 rails. Don, a member of the Dolphins club, turned 120.96 mph in 1948. This car later went "chrome city" and was a top car in the '49 Hot Rod Show.

Kong Jackson's fine '32 roadster. Kong is the guy who made all those fine hot ignitions over the years. He's one of the original members of the Glendale Sidewinders and is still active.

This very fine looking '32 roadster represented the Glendale Sidewinders and was owned by the driver, Walt Noble. Best speed at the time of the photo was 123.96 mph.

Bob Steiger, Oilers club member, ran this hiboy '32 roadster only once after completion, turning 98 mph. Engine was '32 V8 with stock heads, Thickstun manifold, Spalding ignition.

This pretty 239 cu.in. class B streamliner recorded a best speed of 142.18 mph during the 1948 season. The car was owned by Lancers club members Bob Path and Chuck Moore.

Junior Rotter's front-engine C class tank was a point getter for the Dolphins club during the 1948 SCTA season with a top speed of 141.73 mph.

This former ASC track job is being rebuilt by Johnny Van Houten to run the lakes representing the Dolphins club. The '24 T is powered by stock Merc bore block, Eddie Meyer heads and manifold, Meyer ignition and Winfield cam.

Chuck Daigh's 251 cu.in. C class '29 roadster. Engine is a '41 Merc with Navarro heads and manifold, Emery cam and Splading ignition. This engine turned 148.76 mph in a front-engine drop tank in 1948. Chuck was a Dolphins club member.

At "full song" is the Stanford and Lynn 135 cu.in. V8 60 class A engine powering their tank to a 110.02 mph run at El Mirage in 1948. The little 60 ran Ford heads, Meyer manifold, Smith cam and Ford ignition. Club affiliation was Gear Grinders.

This rear-engine '29 roadster ran 126.40 mph with its B class engine on June 6th, 1948. The car was owned and driven by Charles Clark, Santa Ana, California. The 1938 Ford engine was equipped with Meyer heads, Evans manifold, Winfield Super Cam, Arnett ignition.

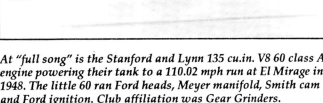

Joe Patterson Jr., future SCTA member, gets started young in the lakes scene. He has just dusted off Jack Morgan's fine red roadster. A 1948 photo.

Kicking up a batch of El Mirage dust is Fred Renoe in his B class (yes, it's listed as a streamliner) at the September 1948 SCTA meet. Fastest speed was 126.76 mph. Fred was a Roadrunner club member.

Bob Riese, Gear Grinders, gets a tow on El Mirage to start his modified roadster.

Roland Mays' (L.A. Gophers) '32 roadster before reworking. The car was completely redone. Updated roadster shows white walls, steel wheels, new top and stock hood sides. Roland's '41 Ford V8 engine running Evans heads and manifold, Weber cam, and Potvin ignition, turned a best speed of 123.97 mph. The engine was built by Taylor and Ryan, custom engine builders.

Road Runner club member, Ray Brown, tunes his rear-engine A roadster on a warm-up run at El Mirage in 1948. Engine is '38 Ford V8-60 with Meyers heads and manifold, own cam and ignition.

A 133 mph time was recorded by the Barber & Dalph '25 T "C" class roadster at El Mirage in 1948. Engine was a '39 Merc with Navarro heads and manifold, Clay Smith cam, and Barker mag.

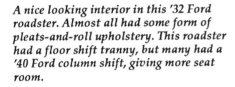

A nice looking interior in this '32 Ford roadster. Almost all had some form of pleats-and-roll upholstery. This roadster had a floor shift tranny, but many had a '40 Ford column shift, giving more seat room.

Ak Miller gives a wave while Harvey Haller, next to pickup, looks on. Ak's roadster lurks in the background. Post WWII.

Junior Rotter's C roadster ran 117.64 mph. Engine was later switched to Junior's "Walking Dog" drop tank and blasted through the course at 141+ mph. (L to R) Bob Rollin, Junior Rotter, Dick Murphy.

Left- Gear Grinder club member S.E. Drake in his full belly-panned '27 T roadster.

'29 Model A pickup owned by Fred Grim. Powered with a B Winfield flathead, Winfield cam, Wico magneto and his own manifold, turned 97.80 mph.

Dick Price's 123.28 mph C class '32 roadster. Ford V8 engine ran Edelbrock heads and manifold, Smith cam and Potvin ignition.

Bob Griffin recorded a 117.64 mph time at a 1948 SCTA lakes meet in his B class '32 roadster. V8 engine ran Meyers heads, Navarro manifold, Cannon cam and his own ignition.

This San Bernardino, CA based '32 C class roadster, owned by Frank Perry, ran 111.11 mph in 1948 on El Mirage dry lake. V8 engine ran Kelly heads and manifold, Winfield cam and his own special ignition. Engine size 3-5/16 bore, stock stroke.

Ralph Weston's "B" class A V8 roadster. Ralph's best speed in 1948 was 103.48 mph, SCTA time, running a '41 Ford block, Merc bore, Thickston 9:1 heads, Evans manifold, Harmon & Collins cam, Jenkins ignition. Under the full race tarp was a neat Auburn dash installation. The Carlsbad Oilers was Ralph's club.

Guptill and Howrd of the Lancers club ran this 248 cu.in. "B" '27 T roadster on '32 rails to a Russetta Timing Association speed of 129.11 mph. The '41 Merc engine ran Evans heads and manifold and Smith cam. Car was also "A" class Russetta record holder with a speed of 125.56 mph.

Above- Wheelers club member Dave Ratliff at full throttle in his "C" class '32 V8 roadster. 116 mph was the best speed attained with his '42 Mercury engine. The Wheelers club started February 10, 1941. Was admitted to SCTA in May, 1941. Disbanded in 1942 because of WWII. Started again in 1946.

Marques and Kimes (Wheelers club members) display their old 3/4 Ascot speedway car. The Ford "B" engine runs Cragar equipment. Look close, a rod and piston are hanging out of the hole in the block.

Here's a beauty! The Bottema Brothers '29 Model A roadster on '32 rails. The superb metal work was done by the old master, Whitey Clayton. The little '29 ran Model B Ford engine with Cragar goodies. Turned 103 mph.

A post-war front-engine belly tank streamliner. Check out the small windshield and front air scoops.

Above- Otto J. Crocker, SCTA chief timer, eyeballs the clock as J.E. Tucker's Riley-equipped 4-banger enters the SCTA traps. El Mirage, 1948.

Here's a drive-up roadster owned by Jean J. Jones, member of the Pasadena Roadsters club. Engine is a Knudsen-equipped Ford six. Ran as a "B" class roadster. How about that laid back front license plate. Was this the start of the race car front wings?

179

A very sharp looking '29 roadster running Herb's Associated, (Glendale, California) sponsorship. The 336 "C" number indicates the owner belongs to the Glendale Sidewinders.

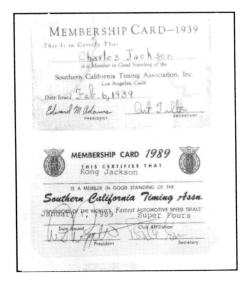

Above- SCTA membership cards belonging to Charles "Kong" Jackson (Kong Ignitions), span 50 years as a member, and still going strong. He is currently manufacturing super strong nitro heads, manifolds and ignitions for, you guessed it, flatheads!

Right- Starting line scene, late '40s SCTA lakes meet. Doug Hartlet, #1R, awaits the starter's "go" signal. #2 car in background is Randy Shinn's record-setting roadster.

An early 21-stud Ford flathead-powered T bobtail gets a last minute going-over before its trip through the traps. How about those rear mechanical brake rods?

Left- The Spalding Brothers streamliner gets the once-over at a pre-war lakes meet. This car was a head turner wherever it appeared.

Above- Star of the TV series "Untouchables", Robert Stack is pictured here in his Cragar-equipped Model B-powered '31 Model A roadster back in the early days of his screen career.

This clean looking "C" modified roadster, driven by LeRoy Titus, ran 151.51 mph at the 1950 Bonneville Nationals. Engine was a 296 cu.in. Merc flathead V8.

During this early 1948 SCTA meet, Paul Schiefer in his very sharp looking "C" class T roadster ran 136.77 mph, powered by a '47 Merc engine with Edelbrock heads and manifold, Harman Collins cam and Meyer Ignition.

Ernie McAfee's streamliner that won the 1938 season champion-
ship. SCTA's first tube-frame car. Engine was a 4-cylinder Ford,
Winfield flathead equipped. Fastest speed: 137.41 mph one way.
Two-way average was 132.89.

Unusual early streamliner. Body looks to be framework covered
by fabric. Ran before the war.

The Vic's Garage tail job waiting in line at Harpers dry lake,
1939-'40.

Model T modified waits to run at a pre-war lakes meet.
Check the hand brake tucked up behind the exhaust pipes.
Grabbing the brake handle was probably a thrill!

Danny Sakai's beautiful modified, pictured here at a lakes
meet back in the good old days — 1940 - '41. Car ran consistently in the 128+ mph bracket. Not too bad for a four-holer.

Another bob-tailed T modified waiting in line to run. Length springs on front — Ford buggy spring on rear. Brakes mechanical, rear only. Modified 4-cylinder power.

Things haven't changed since the early lakes meets. You still wait in line to run, like this Vic's Garage modified driver who is getting his zzz's in this pre-war starting line countdown on Harpers dry lake in 1939.

Who needs a chain hoist or jack stands? The early lakes boys just turned the car up on its side, pulled the pan and tightened up the bottom end.

A few quick tweeks of the carburetors and it's time to go, as the driver vaults behind the wheel, ready for a dusty pass through the pre-war traps. Photo by John Riley.

Right- A nice front end shot of Paul Schiefer's beautiful T lakes roadster. Paul's '47 Merc engine ran Edelbrock heads and manifold, Harmon & Collins cam, Meyer ignition. Ran 136.77 mph in the 1948 season.

Above- Jim Harris' B roadster charges down the lake bed during a post-war SCTA meet. The 239 cu.in. '34 Ford V8 engine ran a 119.04 mph speed with the help of Meyers heads, Edelbrock manifold, Winfield cam and Potvin ignition. Jim was a member of the Hornets club.

A 1948 starting line scene during a SCTA El Mirage dry lake meet. #799b, Arvel Youngblood, Idlers club member, waits his turn.

Don Cox, ready to get down to some serious racing in his channeled '34 roadster. His '46 Merc engine ran Evans heads, Weiand manifold, Cannon cam and his own ignition. Check the camp layout in the background. Not a motel in sight!

Above- The original fat boy, Charles W. "Tiny" Tyler in his Sunday Patrol sedan delivery. Without the patrol cars, a safe lakes meet would be impossible.

The King-Hansen A class streamliner runs a 1939 V8-60 engine with a displacement of 140 cubic inches. Equipped with filled Ford heads, Edelbrock manifold, Winfield cam and Spalding ignition. The best speed for the car was 112.92 mph.

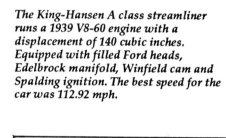

Above- Howard Wilson in Stu Hilborn's streamliner just before making its first 150 mph run.

Right- This highly customized '29 roadster, featuring a V-windshield, special grille and hood turned 115.83 mph with a 239 cu.in. engine. Owner Wes Gardner was a member of the Redlands Hornets club.

Wally Parks, before NHRA, in his '29 street roadster. Wally drove this car to and from his work at Hot Rod Magazine in the early '50s. Picture was shot on the Hollywood Freeway before it was opened to the valley. Oh my, how times have changed!

Left- Phil Remington's super neat "B" class modified. Turned 135.73 mph at a 1948 SCTA meet. Used a '40 Merc engine for power, equipped with filled Ford heads, Navarro intake manifold, Engle cam and Zephyr ignition. Phil was a member of Low Flyers SCTA club.

Dick Rathman at speed in his "Sweet 16" track roadster. Car was a runner both on the roundy round tracks and at the lakes. Jim went on to be one of the Indianopolis 500's top drivers.

Bell Auto Parts-sponsored modified roadster (without modified nose) displaying the stepped-height velocity stacks providing rammed fresh air for each carburetor. Ran strong. Bob Riese, Gear Grinders club member, is the owner.

Fred Oatman waits in line with his V8-powered bobtail modified on a cold morning at the lakes right after the war.

Richard Fugle gets a tow start for his Ford V8-60 powered "A" class roadster. Richard, a Low Flyers club member, turned 104.16 mph at the SCTA meet. Engine ran filled heads, Edelbrock intake, Engle cam, Coon ignition.

Fred Hadley's 4-cylinder Riley "B" class roadster, Chuck Potvin at the wheel. The roadster turned 124.93 mph at El Mirage in 1948.

The San Bernardino SCTA Hornets club's '48 trophy winners. Left to right: Ivan Vipond, Roy Aldrich, C.W. Scott, Junior Tucker, Wes Gardner, LeRoy Holmes, C.W. Tyler and Gordon Patterson.

Phil Remington's 135.73-mph streamliner, sporting a new tail. Phil later worked for Shelby on the Cobras.

Above- An Evans-equipped '32 roadster driver gets a helmet chin strap adjustment from his girlfriend before starting down the course at El Mirage dry lake.

Right- Don Francisco (center) of the Burke/Francisco record-holding (164.83 mph) tank, is hard at work either repairing or changing rear end gears on their belly tank. Engine is a 272 cu.in. '42 Merc with Edelbrock heads and manifold.

Far Right- Veda Orr and Rex Mays (well-known circle track racer) get a demonstration of the merits of McMillan oil by a McMillan Oil representative. Veda was one of the only women to compete at the lakes. Not only did she compete, but she went fast in her "C" roadster. Veda was married to Karl Orr, of Karl Orr Speed Shop fame. Veda, during WWII kept the SCTA newsletter going to all the So-Cal servicemen at home and overseas. This newsletter did more to promote the sport of lakes racing to other parts of the US than any other thing. Her letters and the SCTA newsletter kept all of us servicemen pumped up until the war ended and we could come home and resume racing.

This "B" class streamliner #27B, owned by Arnold Birner, was one of the first 58 car numbers issued from the 1946 championship time trials. These numbers remained throughout the 1947 season.

Bruce Brown's channeled '27 T roadster. A member of the Road Masters club, this little beauty turned 114.50 mph running custom heads, .060" overbore Merc and a Pierce ignition.

Above- Jack Hennessy, a member of the Clutchers club, in his sharp looking '32 roadster. This Navarro-equipped '41 Merc, with a Smith cam, turned a "B" class roadster time of 119.46 mph.

The #720 CS that Stu Harper ran on this car indicates it ran as a streamliner during the '48 season. The streamliner classification was later changed. This '27 T ran full belly pan, "C" class engine of between 250 and 350 cu.in., Weiand heads and manifold, Scintilla mag. Car turned 117.48 mph and was a member of the Road Masters club.

190

This very nice '32 street roadster was owned by Dean Batchelor, SCTA Road Runner club member. Running a "B" class, 239 cu.in. engine equipped with Navarro heads, Smith cam, Edelbrock manifold and Ord ignition, Dean turned 126.58 mph on September 25, 1948.

Harvey Haller's channeled '29 "B" class roadster was consistant top runner in its class during the 1947 season. Engine was a '38 Ford V8 with Evans heads and manifold, Winfield cam and Spalding ignition. Turned 128.57 mph SCTA clocks.

Bottom Left- Randy Shinn's 1946 SCTA record-holding roadster (128.66 mph), and #24, Bert Letner's "Elco Twin" track and lakes T roadster. Car turned a 130 mph one-way pass, Pacific Timing Association, 1947.

Below- The Throttlers club's Pat O'Brien, all saddled up and ready to go in his '"C" class '32 roadster, powered by a '41 Merc with filled and milled Ford heads, Edelbrock manifold, Winfield cam, stock Ford ignition. Best speed in '48 was

Owner Bill Roberts takes time out from his plug changing chores to smile at the camera. His A V8 is powered by a Ford flathead V8 bolted to a pair of Riley OHV heads. Looks like a homemade dual carb manifold.

Above- Stu Hilborn's "B" streamliner getting heavy spectator attention at this 1948 SCTA meet. Holds the class record at 145.640 mph.

Above- Vic Schnackenberg's '29 Model A roadster. Engine is 258.53 cu.in. Merc flathead V8. Turned 122.61 mph at the SCTA meet in 1948.

Don Blair's #57 track roadster. This car ran both the track and lakes. Turned in a quick 124.88 mph, Russetta timing. Buddy Van Mannen drove the roundy round races.

Looks like these guys got it made as they relax while a wife or girlfriend is hard at it painting the car's number and class on this '33 "B" class roadster. Russetta, August 1950.

An SCTA 1947 El Mirage starting line scene. Looks like '32 city! Things haven't changed much over the years. You still have to wait in line to run.

Jim Rathman's CRA track roadster at speed at the old Bonelli Stadium, Saugus, California, 1948. Jim went on to become a top speedway driver, winning the 1960 Indy 500.

1929 roadster with centrifugal blower, slingshot dual manifold and dual electric fuel pumps. Car belonged to Chuck Wright of the Nite Owls club.

A very typical '32 hiboy roadster that ran at the lakes right after WWII. Many of these cars were driven by their owners every day to and from school or work.

Road Master club members, October 1948, Van Nuys Airport, left to right: #723B T V8 114.50 mph, Bruce Brown; #713B Riley 4-port, 109.75 mph, Jack Thompson; #717B Riley V8 OHV, 118.57 mph, Harold Johanson; '29 A V8 owned by Paul Grosso; #720C modified T V8, 117.48 mph, Stu Harper.

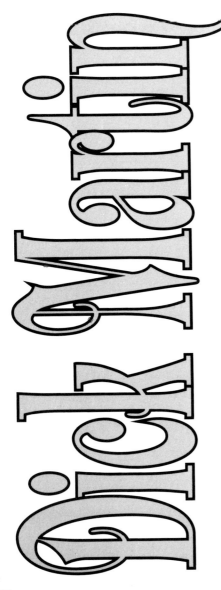

TOM: How did your interest in cars develop. What were your first cars, and how did you hop them up?

DICK: I got my first car in 1941. It was a Model A roadster. You could buy them then anywhere from about $5 to $100. Well maybe not quite that much. There was hardly any speed-equipment thing going on at that time. The first thing I did to my roadster was put a street pipe on. That sounds kind of corny, but that's what was being done in those days. Shortly afterwards I got a dualed drop manifold that I put two 97s on. The car sure as heck ran better then. There were no muffler shops, or that type of thing around. Costs were high compared to income. I was 15 at the time and still in high school.

I had a chance to trade my roadster for a '32 phaeton, with no top. That was the beginning of having my first real hot rod. There was a fellow in Portland, Frank Costanzo, who sold Edmunds equipment and Winfield cams. There was another place in Portland, owned by a fellow named Burke White, who kind of specialized in splitting manifolds and putting dual exhausts and things like that on some cars. Basically it was just a regular garage, but he would do it. My '32 was pretty sad with a '32 engine in it, because the engines weren't very good. I rounded up a really good LB block for it (so it was still 221), and installed a Winfield cam and an Edmunds manifold. I had Frank put the cam in the engine, and I built the heads. That '32 touring phaeton was about the fastest car in town, and I couldn't understand why. I wasn't smart enough to figure out that this car weighed a little less than 2000 lbs. With a cam and carburetor and milled heads, it just went like a scared rabbit.

I acquired a '36 Ford roadster, and a Mercury engine. I switched all the stuff from my '32 into the Mercury. And now I had a 239 in my '36 roadster. I graduated from high school with Randy Francis (who is now a Ford dealer), and Ralph Kirkwood (who became one of the best midget engine builders in the nation). Ralph's engines did some wild things. He was the first one to cut a Chevy V8 in half, only he cut it crossways before he cut it lengthways.

Randy and Ralph and another fellow named Don Siddons and I went to L.A. in the summer of 1943 to find out how things are really done. We ran into Al Swanson, who had Al's Speed Shop on Colorado. We bought some Winfield cams and an Edelbrock manifold for Randy. I went over to the Carson top place and saw them. We chopped the top over at Al's place, and he welded up the posts for us. But, we didn't have the dough to get the Carson top. We also picked up a '33 Ford phaeton for Don. We paid $140 for it. Burned oil like you couldn't believe. When we got back home, we pulled the engine out. He had no money, because he was still a senior in high school. We ported and relieved it. Ralph bored out the Mercury, and we put a new set of used pistons in it, and one of the Winfield cams we bought from Swanson. We milled the heads, and slapped it back in his '33 phaeton.

TOM: How did you get going in the muffler business?

DICK: While we were in L.A., I was most impressed by the Porter Muffler Shop. I got my mother to write to them and get a dealership on the Porter Mufflers. When I got home and we got the dealership, I started loading my garage up with Porter mufflers and putting dual exhaust on everybody's Ford.

I started a chain of muffler shops in Oregon and Washington, and added speed shops to 'em. When I say speed shops, I sold speed equipment. I did not build engines, or anything like that. I did occasionally for friends, but not as a normal procedure.

TOM: You got going pretty heavy in track roadsters along in there, didn't you?

DICK: In '47 the track roadsters were really a big thing, and I jumped into it with both feet. By then I had a boring bar, and was boring holes. And, I sold an awful lot of Jahns pistons, which was a hot number in those days. I was boring engines, porting and relieving them. I was picking up a lot of the old Merc engines, because everyone was replacing their engines with 59s. (59A and 59AB as they were called, but they were really just a 59-block.) And I would pick up all those used Fords and Mercurys, and I was boring a lot of those out. Putting in Jahns pistons and Harmon & Collins cams.

I had my own track roadster, which after about three or four races was kind of top dog around the northwest. That went well until McGrath and Ayulo came up. At that time I was running a '27 T pickup, which was a little on the heavy side with all that steel. And they came up here and proceeded to trounce me. And about that same time, young Fred Offenhauser rolled into town and showed me his Offenhauser heads and manifold. I was really impressed with the workmanship on them. His head was chambered a little bit differently

Fast heat, first race of the 1947 season, May 13th at Portland Speedway's paved 5/8 mile track. On the pole is #57 Don Moore in Al Reamer's '27 T. Outside 1st row is Jim Martin in Tom Storey's #33 channeled A roadster. Second row is #23 Randy Francis in his '32 roadster, #1 Frank McGowen in "Pop" Loch's A V12 (Lincoln Zephyr). Third row has Dick Boubel (#50) '27 T roadster, #14 Dick Martin in the Martin/Ron Jones '27 T pickup. Most of the cars in the Portland area at that time ran Sanafelt heads and manifolds that were made in Portland.

from everyone else's.

The night that McGrath and Ayulo came up to my shop to see my place, I was putting a set of heads and intake manifold on, and taking my old Shanafelt set-up off. The Shanafelt really wasn't very good. It was a single plenum operation, and the heads were just like a lot of the others.

The next day I went out to the races. But I had forgotten to retorque the heads on my car. Although their cars were much faster than mine, we snaked through the main event. And darn, if we weren't winning the race. Then I blew a head gasket because we weren't retorqued. We spun out in our own water, and they won first and second. I didn't even finish.

That really made a change in my life, because I immediately took the car home, and tore it apart, shortened it five inches, shoved the engine back fourteen inches, and put a roadster back half on it. Ended up with it down to 1400 pounds, and immediately went out with it the following Saturday and unofficially broke their track record that I had held all the time before they had come. Then on Sunday, we broke the hell out of it, because I didn't want to be number two. That pretty well finished up the '47 season.

In 1947 Bill Schnell made the first four-carburetor manifolds, to my knowledge. Matter of fact, the Edelbrocks and the Weiands and Sharps and the rest of 'em that came afterwards, I don't think were a nickle's worth better. And they didn't look a heck of a lot different. I think Bill really ought to receive credit for making that first one. Later when they started running the fuels, nitro and things like that, it was imperative that you had the four-carburetor manifold.

TOM: You were known for your work with A-V8s.

DICK: In 1946, the A-V8 was coming of age. There were quite a few of them around, and that was one of my specialties. I used to have a drive-in service. You could drive your Model A in, in the morning, and come back at 5:00 pm and I'd have a V8 in it. (With a set of headers, if you had the money...an extra $25.00. A set of headers and duals already on it, and you could drive it home). That was kind of a specialty. I did most of 'em with '32 cross members, although I did a few with '33 and '34 cross members. And of course, I did some hydraulic brakes.

In '47, I became very prolific in making A-V8s. I had a wrecking yard where I'd buy bodies and frames. Nobody kept a '32 except a roadster and a three-window. All the rest were just junk. Nobody wanted a 2-door, 4-door, or a 5-window coupe. So we'd just turn them on their side, and cut the crossmember out, and we had an A-V8.

TOM: Give us the low-down on how drag racing got its start in the Pacific Northwest.

DICK: Early on, there were several places that we used to drag race around Portland. One of them was out by Lake Oswego. There was a big two-lane road with gravel shoulders, real wide. In those days, there was nothing out there. We used to race there, until we decided either the cops were coming, or they were already there.

Another place was a strip out by Aurora, Oregon, which was about 15-20 miles out of town. It was a beautiful concrete road, with extremely wide gravel shoulders and it had no end. This was kind of a freeway-type of thing. It was built, and it didn't go anywhere. Nobody really knew why. You could race there all night long. There were just a few farmers around, and they never complained. I don't recall the cops ever coming there.

When we had the Oregon Roadster Racing Association, I was vice-president in '46 and '47 and

maybe into '48. When people got interested in drag racing, they were going out to the Aurora Airport, which was closed as an airport. It was an old army or navy emergency base. I went there one weekend and made a plea with the guys, "Let's not drag race here, because it's going to be a problem. We'll see if we can get it ironed out with the law, and maybe we can use this for a dragstrip." About the time I got through with my little speech, down came the state police, the county police and everything, and blocked off all the entrances to it. They made everybody leave. They took everybody's license plate numbers down, but nothing ever came of it.

At the next meeting, the place was packed. All the seats were filled and people were lined up outside. This was the biggest meeting we had ever had. We got around to saying, "Yeah, well, we'll do something about the drag races," but we never did because we were too busy with our own thing, which was making money racing track roadsters.

So, anyway, we missed our chance to be the big shots in drag racing right there. Shortly after that, the Columbia Timing Association was formed, and the Northwest Timing Association was formed. The two of them got going and slowly but surely things took off from there. There got to be airstrips all over the country that were closed and became dragstrips.

I went into drag racing and kind of specialized in automatic transmissions, and especially the Buick engine. I set some records and did different things with them, and finally ended up with an A competition coupe. It blew off my right leg, when the automatic transmission blew up. Until it did, it was a heck of an experiment. For awhile I had two supercharged gassers. One of 'em forced everybody out of the class; it was a 1955 Oldsmobile with a supercharger. The other was a 1955 Buick with a supercharger. They ate everybody alive up here.

Out of that came my little '36 A competition coupe with a Buick Dynaflo set-up in it, supercharged of course. Turned out that the Dynaflo wasn't quite as strong in that '36 as it was in the big '55 Buick. Anyway, it ate me...that might be kind of the end of the story.

The muffler and the speed business made me a multi-millionaire. I owe a lot to it. I've had a lot of fun with it. I guess I should be able to relax and quit now.

There is no fun like that 1941-1948 period. Everybody came home from the service, and they had a little money in their pocket. We had an expanding economy, and the government was not a problem. Everybody was swapping up to new speed equipment. Those were really fun days.

Presently I have a '36 Ford pickup, and a '60 Cad pickup, a Citron Mazerati SM, a Jag XJS, the new Lincoln LSC, a couple of station wagons, three Thunderbird convertibles, two Lincoln convertibles, and three Thunderbird sunroofs (which are very rare). All these cars are not nearly as much fun as those days in '41 to '48, when I usually had only one car, and I was racing.

Dick Martin's '29 roadster is parked in front of his speed shop in Portland. This car ran in roadster races in Oregon and Washington, and finished 5th at the end of the '46 season.

Typical of the era is Joe Hoag's '32 roadster, photographed in 1946.

This is what Portland neighborhoods looked like back in '43. Randy Francis' 1935 roadster with '40 taillights is on the right, and Dick Martin's 1936 roadster is on the left. Both had Carson style tops and door handles removed. The '35 had a V'd windshield.

Portland Speedway, 1947. Car #14 coming in after winning the last race of the season and taking the Oregon Roadster Racing Association championship. Flathead-powered, Offy heads and manifold, Harmon & Collins cam. The car was a pickup at the beginning of the season, then was shortened, lightened and the engine moved back 14 inches.

Portland Speedway, Portland, Oregon, 1947. The Wood Brothers '27 T on '32 rails. Early block, running their own cast aluminum dual manifold.

This once-cherry '29 roadster looks a little worse for wear after a bout with the fence of the 1-1/8 mile dirt track. Yakima, Washington, 1946. Jack Lewis was the owner and driver.

Above-Dick Scandling (Salem, Oregon) drove this 1932 Ford convertible all the way to Yakima, Washington to run the 1946 roadster race on the 1-1/8 mile horse track. Then, if his car was all in one piece, he drove it home again. Oh my!

"Duck" Collins '27 T roadster pickup with "Kuzie" Kuzmanich behind the wheel. Ran the 1947 northwest track season, winning at Aurora Speedway in Seattle, Washington with Gordy Youngstrom (well known midget driver) at the wheel. This car was also driven by northwest Indy and big car driver Les Anderson.

Waiting to qualify on the 1-1/8 mile dirt track in Yakima, Washington is Randy Francis in his fine '32 roadster. Tom Storey, Portland bodyman par excellance, is on the driver's side giving Randy some words of encouragement. Yakima Fairgrounds, 1946.

Louie Sherman, local midget driver, gets set to qualify Dick Scandling's '32 Ford convertible. Early Ford block, Thickstun manifold. Portland Speedway, 1946. Dick Scandling, car owner, is in the baseball cap.

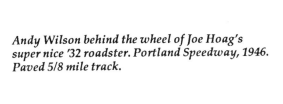

Above-Don Moore driving Al Reamer's '27 T (#57), doing his best to hold off Randy Francis in his '32 (#23) roadster in hard fought trophy dash. Portland Speedway, April 13, 1947.

Andy Wilson behind the wheel of Joe Hoag's super nice '32 roadster. Portland Speedway, 1946. Paved 5/8 mile track.

Gordy Youngstrom qualifying Dick Scandling's '32 convertible at Portland Speedway in 1946. Thickstun manifold, 21-stud block.

Six converted street roadsters sail out of turn four at Portland Speedway during the B roadster racing main event in 1946.

Northwest roadster boys hard at it coming out of turn four at Portland Speedway in 1946. Car with windshield is Dick Scandling's '32 convertible with Louie Sherman driving in the B roadster main event.

Dick Martin and Ron Jones owned car #14. This photo shows the car rebuilt after a crash in the first race of the '47 season. The car went to Seattle that night and won the main event at Aurora Speedway with Allen Heath driving.

Above-Don Siddon's '33 Phaeton has a '34 front end, ported and relieved '33 engine with Merc bore and Winfield cam. Exterior features a Carson style top and DeSoto bumpers.

Winter of '46 in Portland. Dick Martin's '29 A-V8 in front, and Ron L'Abbe's '29 A-V8 in background. Both had custom headers. Note split wishbones on Dick's car.

The '39 Merc engine in Dick's car had Shanafelt heads and manifold, Harmon & Collins cam, was ported and relieved. This car ran 5th in points for the '46 season in the Oregon Roadster Racing Association.

Dick Martin comes in after qualifying #13 on the Yakima 1-1/8 mile dirt track in 1947.

This is pretty typical of the flathead V8 set up for racing, installed in a '29 roadster. The photo was taken at the Yakima track in 1947.

Here's the '29 A-V8 roadster stripped for racing in Yakima, Washington in 1947. Note the clod-catching radiator screen.

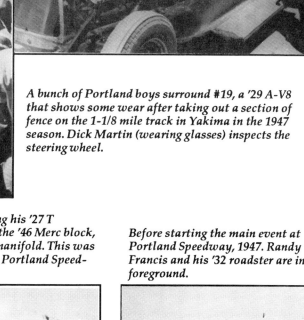

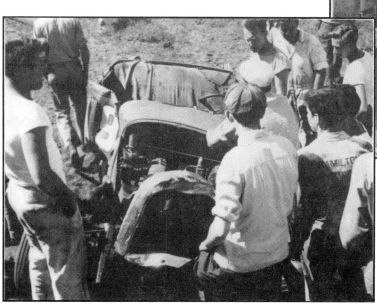

A bunch of Portland boys surround #19, a '29 A-V8 that shows some wear after taking out a section of fence on the 1-1/8 mile track in Yakima in the 1947 season. Dick Martin (wearing glasses) inspects the steering wheel.

The helmet dash at Portland Speedway in April of 1947 had Don Moore in Al Reamers #57 '27 T, while Jim Martin drove Tom Sturey's #33 channeled '30 A. Randy Francis drove his '32 hiboy.

Dick Martin qualifying his '27 T roadster pickup with the '46 Merc block, Shanafelt heads and manifold. This was in April of 1947 at the Portland Speedway.

Before starting the main event at Portland Speedway, 1947. Randy Francis and his '32 roadster are in the foreground.